# PAUL SÉDIR

*His Life and Work*

# PAUL SÉDIR

*His Life and Work*

⊕

FRIENDS
IN SPIRIT

First published in French as *Sédir Mystique*
Éditions des Amitiés Spirituelles, 1957
First English edition, © Friends in Spirit, 2024
an imprint of Sophia Perennis
Translation © Friends in Spirit 2024
Series Editor: James R. Wetmore

For information, address:
Friends in Spirit
Box 931, Philmont, NY 12565

ISBN 978-1-59731-237-0 (pbk)
ISBN 978-1-59731-238-7 (cloth)

Cover Design: Michael Schrauzer

# CONTENTS

# PART III
## LETTERS

# Acknowledgments

The publisher is deeply indebted to the "friends" of *Les Amitiés Spirituelles*, who have kept Paul Sédir's books in print in French for over a century, and for the dedication of those who have nurtured the vision that one day these books might appear in worthy editions for Anglophone readers. We gratefully thank in this connection Piers Vaughn and Peter Urbanski for the exchange of textual materials many years ago that led to this presents series, Robert Ledwidge for his technical assistance, and especially Madame Zadah Guérin-McCaffery, who nurtured this same vision and worked towards its realization for decades. Her skilled devotion to Sédir's works helped ensure that Sédir's carefully crafted style has been preserved in these Friends in Spirit translations.

# PART I

## Short Biographies by Two Friends

*Max Camis*
*& Émile Besson*

# Paul Sédir:
## by Max Camis

PON THE HILLOCKS bathed by the Rance River, the ancient city of Du Guesclin preserves numerous vestiges of feudal times in the ogival arches of its thick ramparts. It was in one of the poorest abodes along the rue de la Lainerie, in the network of its medieval lanes with its corbelled and sculpted homes, close to the marketplace reeking with the pungent odors of the fishmongers, that the young Yvon Le Loup was born. In the usual bureaucratic jargon, the birth certificate dryly declares, "thus it is stated upon the registries in the said parish of Dinan, that one Yvon Le Loup by name, son of Hippolyte and Séraphine Foeller, was born January 2, 1871 at 3 o'clock in the afternoon."

Our friend Sédir, who was far too reticent to reveal much of himself, rarely spoke of his childhood. However, some pages written later in life offer clues of his first impressions of Armorica[1] and its grand past, wherein he describes with emotion the depths of the forest Brocéliande, where the enchanter Merlin died. The drama of the setting must have left a deep impression upon his soul as a child. Details from this period are unfortunately lacking, and we will not attempt to romanticize them. To embellish the impecunious life of a woman obliged to leave her native land and relocate with a small child in tow to a city foreign to her; to

[1] Brittany.

1

embroider upon the life of a father who, as a regular soldier had, to undergo all the fatigues and privations at the end of a war[2] that had been so hard for our side, would be too facile. However, most historians claim that in the life of certain great men, the influence and role of a mother are all important. We will look forward to returning to this leitmotif, but for the moment it is the little boy with whom we are concerned.

While others are exuberantly taking their first steps and vibrating to the first awareness of life, he waits in his little iron bed, already resigned to a more difficult ordeal: a painful condition attributable to a latent tuberculosis that the family's privations had accentuated. And these doldrums dragged on that much the longer owing to the menial situation. The still meager salary of the parents did not permit better care; on the contrary, presaged worse to come. For a long time even his eyes were at risk. A near total blindness necessitated medical care. Then it happened that, while looking at the large letters on the chart in the shop of the optician examining him, the poor child, not being accustomed to the vertical position, took a fall that caused the first fracture of his leg. We can well commiserate with his enduring, long, lonely days and the complications of life brought about by the conditions of a bedridden child moving thereafter from one to another poor Parisian lodging.

To engage his reflective and avid mind, his studies began quite early. Upon the little board installed across the bed, dramas of spilt inkwells alternated with his determined calligraphic efforts. Mme Le Loup told us how people were surprised to see such beautiful penmanship. As time went

---

[2] The Franco-Prussian War, 1870–1871.

on, his handwriting became more and more elegant, and its clarity drew the attention of all who saw it.[3] The harmonious curves penned upon white vellum were later to express so many words—such inspired and consoling thoughts, reflections of the great soul of our friend!

Owing to the Hessian origins of his mother, he learned the German language from birth—not only to speak, but to write it easily—for at the age of fifteen he undertook a translation of Goethe's memoirs.[4] It might well be due to this text, and later to the novel *Wilhelm Meister*, wherein Goethe gives us to understand his mysterious researches and subsequent encounters, that the ferment of occult sciences started to develop in Sédir's mind.

After the war of 1870, M. Le Loup, reduced to a meager military pension and having no other trade, found himself obliged to take a position as a butler in the Pare Monceau district and park his little family in various lodgings in the Batignolles quarter.

Due to his mother's religious principles, the boy probably had his first contact (as soon as his health permitted) with a program of study in the library of the neighborhood school. This program could never be followed faithfully on account of the usual childhood diseases, along with recurring injuries to his leg that frequently confined him to his room. These studies suffered the effects of such accidents all the more in that, owing to such chaotic beginnings, thoughtful natures such as his often have a rather slow comprehension and adaptiveness. The quartier or district was then rather

---

[3] Dr Carton, in his book on human signatures, takes the one of Sédir as a model and example of wisdom.

[4] *Wahrheit und Dichtung* (Truth and Fiction).

secluded from the center of business and noise, consisting mainly of small investors receiving annuities, along with artists and composers who had had their day and were living amid these calm surroundings. From time to time the local omnibus, pulled by its large white horses, would rumble heavily over the rounded cobblestones, after which silence would fall again upon the small private homes nestling in their gardens, and upon the houses then being built. The little boy, already solemn, would dreamily walk along, dragging his leg through these provincial streets.

Sédir often spoke to us of the first project of his youth, of his desire to become a shepherd, to lead into the heather and thyme his sheep and ewes guarded by a dog. In a charming chapter published in this present book ("The Little Shepherd") one finds the nostalgia of this sickly child desiring space and escape. To lead his flock! Has he not achieved it on a broader plane, in a decor not only calm but at least on a more grandiose scale? Dreams and anguish at the beginning are often, for children, a precursive vision of the future. They are transpositions, fine-tunings that harsh fate imposes, and life passes in regret of an unrealizable dream. Yet, seen from the standpoint of eternity, dreams and reality have often been intertwined without the lesson being well understood! Between the child Yvon and Sédir the inspired leader of a School, there is little difference, since—such was the will of God—he understood the modification of his childhood dream.

Now, although the relationship may be awkward on principle, and if a cross-checking of memories is correct, in 1882 the Le Loup household was engaged by a single lady who lived halfway up the rue du Rocher. This better remunerated position made it possible for the young Yvon to take violin lessons—and he played rather well. But, to note a rather peculiar lack in this extraordinarily endowed being, gifted in so many ways, he did not have a good ear.[5]

Regarding his religious formation, changing parishes brought him to catechism classes at the Church of Saint-Augustin, at that time still jubilant with gilt, gold, and freshly remounted frescoes. Although the atmosphere of such a new sanctuary was hardly propitious to the blossoming of a pious soul, we know that the young catechumen threw himself heart and soul, and with assiduous conviction, into his studies. After his first communion, the health of the schoolboy improved. Vacation over, the family had to think of having him continue his education in a serious institution, as all who knew him felt it imperative that he do so. In spite of required heavy expenditures and sacrifices, they thought of the École des Francs-Bourgeois, then one of the best religious education schools in Paris.

The venerable building housing this school (designed by Ducerceau for the Duke of Mayenne), having been at one time or another the center of the conspiracies of the Ligue, then the Favard school in the eighteenth century, had finally been taken over in 1850 by the Brothers of Christian Doctrine. Situated in the Faubourg-Saint-Antoine, where each stone speaks of a past of ostentation and riots, this center of learning must have been of interest to the sensitive mind of the young boy entering his thirteenth year. The teaching, led by Father Argémir de Jésus, was remarkable. Moreover, along with the program there was the stim-

[5] Though loving music, having even composed an Our Father, he had to give up the violin about 1906, having by then realized that he would always lack a good ear.

ulation of brilliant literary groups in which the young Le Loup shortly thereafter distinguished himself.

But one wintry day, upon the trench-like gullies transformed into slides, our myopic little friend, unable to gauge the danger, fell again and broke for the second time his ill-starred leg. Long, dismal, gloomy days followed, but he filled his time with reading the Fathers of the Church. Sédir told us how he filled notebook after notebook with reflections and precious commentaries regarding dogmas, without any of the professors being the wiser.

Twenty years later, after having sought out and probed all states of human thought, after having studied all religious forms and penetrated all initiatory arcana—having "looped the loop" of knowledge—he returned to this theme of faith, to amplify it, to illuminate it with that wonderful inspiration which the early years had already seemed to sense.

Just as Pascal rediscovered the great mathematical principles, Sédir too, very early in life, felt the breath of the gospels, the influence of the great certitudes permeating the metaphysical domains.

⊕

On par with the secret garden of Sédir's thoughts, among the conscientious studies he undertook at the Francs-Bourgeois School, sketching was a subject he especially favored and cultivated even after leaving school. A close observer, he mastered the skill of line drawing, enabling him to make an adroit pen-and-ink sketch of a head, design an *ex libris* for his friends, or sketch the various attitudes of his dogs. To the early childhood dream of becoming a shepherd, the hope of someday becoming a painter was secretly added. Literature, music, and drawing became enthusiastic youthful projects, bequeathing the mature man, by turns, a most rich palette of resources. He was always extraordinarily clever with his hands. Often he told his close friends how much he would have wanted to be a "bricoleur" (jack-of-all-trades). The living, minute description of Andreas's workshop, found in the first chapters of his later autobiographical work *Initiations*, conjures up the framework in which he would have liked to live. But, following a well-known law of restraint, the adolescent had to renounce *en bloc* all these beautiful dreams, to find himself confined for long years to come, after the summer vacation that followed his final examinations.

Having timidly presented his hopes and wishes to his father, the latter, a disciplined old soldier still bound and restrained by his menial job, did not even entertain the matter. His practical and positive state of mind could not comprehend the refined sensitivity of his introverted, quiet son, still less the high aspirations concealed from view. And so, while youth often seems most uncompromising and lashes out at restraints—often rebelling against directives already abraded by suffering and reflexions—our young man docilely took the path of the Banque de France, where he remained, for twenty years, in the same department of stocks, bonds, and securities, without resorting to any schemes or intrigues in view of advancement. Taking his talents and qualities into consideration (and we must admit his being ambitious by nature), one can only explain this fact as owing to the orientation of an already profound interior life. The very few recollections we were able to amass from friends and bank officials cite his cordiality and ever-present good mood. The report of one bank supervisor answering a request for references, wrote of Sédir: "Agent giving remarkable services, an expeditious, hard worker in spite of frail health and the hindrance caused by one of his legs, which he had to keep extended beneath his desk."

After having passed a strenuous competitive examination, the date of the admission of Yvon Le Loup as agent was to begin on October 28, 1892. His assigned sector was in the Ventadour Annex, close to the ancient Hotel de Toulouse.[6] This annex, built in the eighteenth century for Italian opera performances, had housed and heard all the stars of song, and drawn all of elegant Paris society. From all that glory, nothing now remained but a monotonous labor of figures, from 9 a.m. to 6 p.m., relieved only by one hour for lunch. At noon, off came his lustrine sleeves, and the young Le Loup would sally forth toward the cour du Louvre, the Seine, and its quays. There, along the parapets of the river, totally free from constraints, he would ferret around in the boxes open to the avidity of bibliophiles, and read while munching a frugal meal. At that time, the hunt could still be fruitful, and for a paltry sum the rare book providence had "accidentally" placed within reach became yours. What lucky moments for the young student ablaze with thirst for knowledge, finding the answer to latent questions. Coincidences? Luck? For us, who recognize the importance that little events such as these may have at the beginning of a life like the one we are here delineating, we detect the hand of God preparing His servant.

Reserved, distant by nature, having but few friends, Sédir told us how, on the few Sundays when Mme Le Loup permitted him to go out, and in the evenings when for some

---

[6] *Hotel* here means a large private residence, usually known as *hotel particulier*: a townhouse.

reason or other he could escape for a few hours, he would spend them with a comrade who roomed in the vicinity of the Institute. There one read untransportable books, and also those that parents would have disapproved of—not because of their moral insufficiency, but because of their heterodox character. These escapades were a constant cause of torment for the mother, always anxious over the health of her "dear little one" (which term she will use up to her death)—so much the more so, as his nature had been particularly quiet so far. She would then remonstrate, warn him against these "girls who are too forward," who pervert youths and lead them to perdition! Reprimands he listened to with a bowed head. But as soon as could be, he would isolate himself in his chilly little room, where his critical sense and rare intuition (that often led to clairvoyance) shielded him from such byways and errors characteristic of young enthusiasts.

Limited by time and means of purchase for lack of funds, for the first two years he would simply absorb most of what he found. Added to the joy of discovery, of annotating, this intellectual clearing-away still remained very difficult. He had to recast, alone, what others do in secondary studies. Fortunately for us, however, the classical structure of his cultural formation did not prevent him from being drawn toward certain (still imprecise) concordances that he fathomed in the domains of symbolism and esotericism. That is why he felt attracted to some of the last of the Romantics: Villiers de l'Isle-Adam, Barbey d'Aurevilly, Gustave Flaubert, Honoré de Balzac; and particularly toward some of their more philosophical stories, which influenced his own early writings. His quest for a definite style, his search for the exact terminology, led him even to correct himself in the midst of giving a lecture. He professed that no matter how feeble it may be, the thought of a man may, by the chain of appropriate words, explain a part of the Absolute. For him, this quest was to remain a lifelong preoccupation, especially when it came to expressing the inspiration sometimes accorded him.

The series of novels (*La Decadence Latine*) by Péladan[7] particularly influenced our young seeker because, aside from the documentation and originality of these studies on customs and morals, certain aspects of the "marvelous" incited him to write a letter of admiration to the author, at the same time asking for an interview. Nothing remains to us of that encounter. But we do know that, wearing his black hair long and curly, his beard Assyrian-style, and draped in violet pleats, Péladan would receive his guests seated upon an elevated armchair, wanting to be addressed as "Sar," in connection with the Rosicrucians. This spectacular window-dressing did not impress our young friend; rather, the contact with this peculiar erudite led him into a minefield. This encounter marked the decisive turn of the works Sédir was to undertake in the domain of what are called the occult sciences. He also took away from the meeting, along with a few books by Éliphas Lévi and Fabre d'Olivet, the address of a study center.

⊕

It was late in the day in the year 1890 that the life-orientation of the young Le Loup took a precise turn. Not far from

---

[7] Joséphin Péladen (1858–1918), French novelist and Rosicrucian who later joined the Martinist order led by Papus (Dr Gerard Encausse). His father was a journalist who had written on prophecies and professed an esoteric-aesthetic form of Rosicrucianism and universalist Catholicism.

the Banque de France, at 29 rue de Trévise, was a bookshop known as the Librairie du Merveilleux, the back room of which was used as a lecture hall, and where for fifty cents a day it was possible to peruse the classics of Hermeticism. But owing to an overdose of timidity that he had to struggle to overcome, he had not dared enter. The recommendation issued by Péladan, however, assuaged his fears, permitting him to meet the publisher, Lucien Chamuel, who, a few years older than he, welcomed him affably. At their first meeting they discussed a few authors and as well the *modus operandi* with which Papus[8] inspired his entourage.

Papus, who was known as the popularizer of the occult sciences, had just terminated his military service. And even while finishing his medical thesis, he still found time to write an impressive number of treatises, which Chamuel, a recent friend, faithfully published. Several of these had already been reprinted. The association between the two became more and more beneficial. It was arranged, then, that at the next meeting between Sédir and Chamuel, Papus would be present.

Many of the publications describing this meeting have mentioned how the divergent natures of Sédir and Papus must have seemed rather odd. The one was tall, ungainly, not knowing what to do with his long, thin arms. His clothes were ill-fitting, especially for a bank employee. Quite careless of style or dress, and beardless, he seemed younger even than his nineteen years. His hair was parted unevenly—not in the two sleek masses (as we later saw

---

[8] Gérard Encausse (1865–1916), whose esoteric pseudonyms were Papus and Tau Vincent, was a French physician and popularizer of occultism, who founded the modern Martinist Order.

him), but by a undefinable part on the left, occasioned by stubborn locks with spiky, rebellious tufts. His skin was grayish and oily and, as is often the case at that age, constellated with pimples, which he kept scratching. His gaze, rather strange due to the divergence of two enormous black pupils which in turn became visible or shaded off under the half-shut lids (the blinking of the near-sighted), remained always peculiar. Lastly, from this not particularly appealing physiognomy, at first sight hardly prepossessing, there nevertheless emanated something unusual and engaging that held one's attention.

A few photographs taken at that time marked the contrast there might have been between him and the young physician Papus, short and thick-set, jovial, extroverted, and, owing to his Spanish ancestry, seeming older than his twenty-five years. With a mustache and beard, mounted on a haughty and kinky head (with something of the look of a Kalmyk Mongol), rather flashingly dressed, the whole gave an impression of strength and decisiveness. The youthful Sédir spoke slowly and kindly in a rather deep, low-pitched monochord voice, accompanied with a somewhat artless smile. Papus, on the other hand, spoke with a well modulated voice, and although by nature profoundly kind and good, his emphasis drifted easily to the authoritarian, often the roguish.

Despite their contrasting natures, Papus took an instant liking to this tall, timid, and clumsy young man. He immediately felt his good will, and was surprised at the breadth of his knowledge, especially his already individualistic judgment. For the services he offered to render, the young bookkeeper, taken at his word, came for several weeks near the square d'Anvers to square away the books, pamphlets, and documents that the rather bohemian-inclined doctor had neglected to put in order.

Then came the hordes of acquaintances. Papus had him meet Charles Barlet, who possessed an encyclopedic erudition, then Gaboriau, Jules Lermina, Paul Adam, Emile Gary de Lacroze, Victor Emile Michelet, Julien Lejay, Marc Haven, and numerous others who had already attained a certain standing—some of them quite renowned. No one paid much attention to the "little clerk with a gimpy leg." But they did see to it that he came along one evening to 21 rue Pigalle to visit Stanislas de Guaita, whose published scholarly works already placed him among the masters. A powerful figure, this renowned, short-set Lorrain, friend of Maurice Barrès, living alone in the midst of magical vocations, of dreams, and possessor of the most complete initiatory library ever assembled in one place. A dilettante without pretensions, descended from a family of men of letters, an "erudite," de Guaita, more of a thinker than a doer, had however conceived a Rosicrucian fraternity (one more added to others!) to be composed of six Unknowns, whom one could call forth from the spirit world, and of six other Brothers who would meet monthly at his comfortable and luxurious abode.

This visit impressed our young friend Yvon. On the other hand, the magus himself felt curiously attracted to this silent student. And so, probably anticipating what the future held, he opened wide his sanctuary, granting permission to work there. This was a considerable gift to a young person who just two years previously was ferreting out books along the quays. Just like the prospectors of California panning ore in hopes of "striking gold," so did Sédir suddenly find himself surrounded with all he could ever hope for—an opportunity immediately made good use of, as just then Papus, submerged beneath so many activities, demanded from his circle of friends articles for the journal *Initiation*, of which he was director.

And they responded. One month after Sédir's acceptance at the rue de Trévise, there appeared "Experiments in Practical Occultism," the first article signed "Le Loup." He had forged on, full steam ahead! Immediately, the demanding editor-in-chief directed him to give a talk—a far more difficult task, taking into consideration the complexities already mapped out. But as worthwhile effort had always been for Sédir his sole reason for living—and the first step being the one that counts—one evening, before a small audience, he made his debut. Having carefully proofread his discourse and arranged his attire, he read (or rather, stammered through) a dense discourse on "Divinatory Sciences and Chiromancy." Everyone, the lecturer included (so one has heard), was happy when it came to an end. And later, in spite of his admirable tenacity, and in spite of training himself daily in speech-making, it must be admitted that the art of oratory never became his.

According to his own morphological system, Papus the physician classified him among the "melancholic willfuls." Aware of his powerful sense of work, and his comprehension of the most difficult problems, Papus asked him to take the secretariat in hand, and also to become a "Martinist." This group of men, reviving the ideas and the kabbalistic rites of Martinez de Pasqually, had just renovated and formed the first unitary grade of the Rosicrucian fraternity of de Guaita. De Guaita had laid the foundations, and as Venerable of the Supreme Council, read the discourse upon Sédir's reception—which took place with great pomp at his home. The ceremony unfolded along the lines of the ritual of the ancient Masonic lodges. At the end of the eighteenth century, the Portuguese Jews had created a lodge known as "Hermanubis," and as our recipient never did anything by halves, he decided to learn all about the doctrine and the works of Louis-Claude de Saint-Martin,[9] whose fraternity he now belonged to.

It is in one of Saint Martin's least known works, entitled *Le Crocodile*, that our neophyte came to be particularly affected by a certain personage—symbolizing the man of faith—whom the author called "Sédir." This anagram of *désir* (desire), with its concise Oriental flavor, its graphic form, and especially its spirit, had fascinated him; and as it was customary among young authors of that time to choose a pseudonym (Encausse had become Papus, Lalande had became Marc Haven, etc.), so, in order to separate himself from the needy life of the punctual employee, the new Martinist chose as his the name Sédir. From that moment on, all his articles in the journals *Initiation*, *Le Voile d'Isis*, and others, were signed "Sédir," as well as his books, which in due course Chamuel would publish.

These two short syllables, which immediately attracted attention, will, throughout the various periods of his life, incarnate the "perfect desire" of obeying the will of God—and, whatever his detractors might think, of forgetting his own interests in favor of making the total sacrifice of his person.

---

[9] Louis-Claude de Saint-Martin (1743–1803), the "Unknown Philosopher," was the creator of a system of "pure spirituality" and follower of the doctrines of Martinez de Pasqually in the nineteenth century.

⊕

This period of effervescence in the revival of occult sciences will in the end be but a way of passage for Sédir. These glittering games of the intellect and of knowledge will not prevent his perceptive awareness from always choosing the most difficult path, so as to follow his destiny—the orientation of which he was not yet able to comprehend.

Having been born poor, of humble parentage, with a debilitating state of health leaving him fragile for long periods, an unprepossessing outer appearance, a limited education, and working at a monotonous job that could engulf him, he finds himself all of a sudden in the midst of a Pleiades of men of science, of letters, of action, reuniting certain primal laws, laws that humanity loses and rediscovers alternately. It is evident that our positivistic twentieth century may smile indulgently, at best, at these spiritual organizations, at these "consecrations" with their "initiatory degrees" devoid of any immediate or official value. But, thinking more about the relativity of all things, is it not possible to admit that these idealists, far from being revolutionary, or desirous of giving themselves a cadre or a framework, do arrive—in the metaphysical realm—at creating values and recapturing symbols far less dangerous than most political calls to action?

Though attracting but a small minority, the need was no less felt during this period. The example given by these few men attracted the unselfish zeal of a whole phalanx of sincere students. It even became necessary to extend the venue for gatherings: meetings, correspondence, and publications were overflowing the bookshop of the rue de Trévise. Chamuel found it necessary to expand and take a new locale at 70 Faubourg Poissonnière. There, Sédir became a more and

more indispensable member of the household: his place in
the dining room was always set, his bedroom always ready,
whenever an urgent or unforeseen event delayed him far
into the night.

As soon as the bank closed, he would arrive to expedite
mail to foreign countries, to receive transient subscribers, to
greet people in quest of information. In his pockets, mixed
with notes scribbled at odd moments on loose papers (a
habit he kept all his life), one would find an article to be
finished, documentation to be looked up, proof sheets to be
corrected for the *Almanach du Magiste*[10] (the first issues of
which, in collaboration with Papus, he had just begun publishing), and also those for his first work, *Les Tempéraments
et la Culture Psychique*, which was coming out shortly.

At dinner, they would go one flight up, and while chat-
ting and smoking a pipe, he and the friends who felt drawn
to this atmosphere would continue working at the dining-
room table. Whenever he was not detained either by a class
or a lecture, he would go back home to 4 rue l'Opéra,
where his parents were then living. On the sixth floor he
had a small room filled with books, files, and other records.
Hanging above his narrow day-bed was a large red embroi-
dery with Hebrew and astrological signs, which, in the zeal
of a beginner, he thought indispensable to the illumination
of his short nights. These are some of the delightful vagaries
of youth, in whatever field may be, from which no one is
exempt.

But this period in the Grands Boulevards sector could
not last. There was a rumor, regarding subterranean excava-

---

[10] This *Almanach* was published for five consecutive years. It contained a whole series of studies on ancient works.

tions for the Métro, of razing houses for the Boulevard Haussmann. Chamuel, not a speculator at heart, did not want to wait to be expropriated. Moreover, Papus and his friends felt strongly drawn to the Left Bank, where one feels the soul of France, the Europe of old. Moving commenced. Two locations were chosen: the ground floor at No. 4, and an apartment at rue de Savoie.

⊕

And so we come to the year 1895. Papus had written and passed his medical thesis brilliantly, and then married. Having opened a private convalescent hospital at Auteuil, he now has less free time. But his heart is set on giving two classes per week at his Faculté des Sciences Hermétiques, as well as lectures at the Sociétés Savantes. On the other hand, Sédir, in full command of all his faculties, assumes the heavier task. Each evening he gives: lessons in Hebrew and Sanskrit (both of which he had by then mastered), from which he develops the ethnic genius, and especially the dual meaning, found in their symbolism and kabbalah; a course upon the soul-training of Hindu fakirs along with various systems of yoga; finally, general studies on ancient civilizations in their planetary and social aspects—not to mention experimental alchemy, astrology, sociology, and all branches of symbolism, which he favored particularly. With the admirable assistance of other directors, he organized research groups in which each student could develop, according to his taste, an aptitude towards hypnotism, magnetism, or even spiritualism.

This idealistic, entirely sincere awakening, centered upon these two young leaders, grew further, extending to foreign lands; whereas concurrently, the Martinist lodge grew more secretly, necessitating the creation of a new lodge, that of the *Sphinx*.

So deeply involved in helping Papus (whom he liked, and to whom he owed much), Sédir, who could perceive quickly right through any situation, could not delude himself any longer regarding these activities. In fact, his articles, his first published works, give some inkling of the dilemma in which he found himself—wanting, that is, to reconcile the domain of secret sciences with mysticism, which latter very definitely attracted him. The first fires of enthusiasm abating, his aristocratic appreciation for the spirit made him understand the importance of an "elect" in whatever field it might lie. Yet, being interested in all fields of life, during his free hours he went along with friends, from the wine cellars of the Halles[11] to the thundering meetings of anarchists and of the first socialists. His particular bent for beautiful literature made him seek out in the Latin Quarter the Brasseries, where literary clans would meet. And still better, the miserable tavern where, amid smoky stalls on Wednesday nights, one could find Verlaine surrounded by his admirers.[12] Most of the time the great poet, sunk morosely into the chair before his absinthe whitened with brandy (which he pompously called his "dynamite") remained silent. But on other evenings, becoming lyrical, he would recite to whoever wished to listen his most beautiful verses on "Sagesse" (Wisdom).

Once a week, the directors of the Lodges met at the house

[11] Cafes in the basements around the Halles, the large wholesale market of Paris, now destroyed.

[12] Paul Verlaine (1844–1896), French lyric poet who influenced the Symbolist School.

of de Guaita, who had recently moved to Avenue Trudaine. He offered them a special mixture of Chinese teas. They spent agreeable hours discussing systems and points of view dear to each member. From time to time, in order to break up paradoxes, the Docteur would throw out a joyous sally that afforded the host, always cautious, the opportunity of redirecting the discussion. Sédir, on the other hand, who never could waste his time, would be perusing old grimoires, always in search of the work that could help him further. Yet he never missed a chance of participating through a well-placed word with the general hilarity. This particular and prodigious gift of being able to do several things at the same time always amazed his friends. To follow through on a very difficult question, to add up figures, to calculate interminable sums (which he brought from the bank)—all the while carrying on a conversation—was a customary habit of his. Over and above his remarkable intelligence and lucidity, he could easily realize concurrent capacities to an extraordinary degree—for example, being able to play several games of chess while wearing a blindfold.

Regarding these evenings of our youth, who hasn't kept fond memories of them! Each man recalling that which gave him the greatest pleasure. Hence the nights were spent tirelessly, one friend accompanying another home upon the sonorous asphalt during calm hours and through deserted streets under a star-studded sky—until the time came for office or clinic hours to recommence.

The meetings of the new Lodge took place on the mezzanine of a little café on rue de l'Ancienne-Comédie. There Sédir came in close contact with Charles Barlet who, due to his English acquaintances, had enticed him to become a member of the Hermetic Brotherhood of Luxor. Then

Marc Haven facilitated his entering into the F.T.L., of which he was one of the founders.

Sédir had previously affiliated himself with the Gnostic Church, in which, under the name of T Paul, he had been consecrated under the honorific and sonorous title of Bishop of Concorezzo. Thriving in the apparent analogy of doctrines, this extraordinary mind, not in the least seduced (indeed, quite to the contrary) by the mirage of the East and its teachings of old—that is, to find its rhythm again by digging into a thousand wells, into a thousand sources, and testing their resistance and their limitations—decided to go on ahead and forge his passage...

On one of the top floors of 5 rue de Savoie, a quiet and retired nook had been fitted up for magical evocations. De Guaita had traced the protective circle and spoken the customary formulas. Regarding these dangerous experiments, we will say nothing, except to quote a thought of Sédir's assuring us that: "It is, here on earth, that for which we pay the most dearly." In a less obscure domain, his alchemical experiments permitted him to rediscover the basis of what is called the "Great Work." These details of the secret life of our friend demonstrate primarily his particular concern for truth, which made him experience everything before being willing to speak of it. Secondly, they show how Sédir, having attained the highest summits of knowledge and powers, was wise enough to break away from them as soon as he realized how worthless they were—and how dangerous.

⊕

With the regular step of the mountain climber who neither hurries nor stops, nor displays any effort, "our good Sédir" (as many of his friends were beginning to call him) was marching up the path. One felt him engrossed in recalling, in reviving, ancient conquests. He was advancing toward a goal (in fact, *the* goal) with giant steps. According to notes he left, it seems he was approaching it on a certain Sunday of July, 1897. Though that particular day did not bring any immediate results, nevertheless it must be considered as the one, just as there is one in which each of us has played a role that has marked all the remainder of our lives. He described it in this manner:

> I was with Chamuel when a special delivery from Encausse came, telling us to come immediately, in order to have the chance of meeting Andreas. At Auteuil, the children told us that he had left, but that he would take the 7 p.m. train at the Lyon station. Convinced that we were running a wild-goose chase, we went to the station. There we found him, with his family and the Encausses. I saw a short, rather thick-set man, with a ruddy complexion, a heavy moustache, dressed neatly but simply. His wife and daughter were dressed without style. Smoking a clay pipe, he was carrying a shoulder bag and had an ordinary thick cane. He was going to and fro without haste, speaking as a good family man. Mme Encausse introduced me, telling him that the natural aptitudes and gifts that I evinced would arouse his interest. He extended his hand with great cordiality, though his glance briefly told me: "This young man is not as extraordinary as they claim," but he voiced the reply: "So, you want me to take care of this young man!"

The train was leaving. Sédir could hardly say a few words to this personage, who was talked about in a surprising and often extraordinary manner, and who, as he expressed it, had just seemed to be a "good family man."

The poetry of the East often evokes the neophyte going to the spring before the reflected images of the great sacred lake to meet the master. Here was but a railroad platform, hustle and bustle, and train whistles. As if nothing had happened, Sédir, seemingly equable, went on at his steady pace, though the inner conflict remained constant.

To a few very close friends he admitted having remained in a state of furor during a whole month without being able to settle down. For those who knew him well, some imperceptible changes in the inflections of his voice, some particular nervous tics in the left cheek, indicated the repressions of this nature who was really authoritarian and demanding, but who to other people seemingly remained calm, placid, even jovial, jocular, disposed to jesting, though never formulating any judgement.

At the bank—amid its turbulence, its frictions, its constant injustices—the monotonous labor had had a fair share in the grinding-down of his self; yet he, accomplishing his task scrupulously without wasting a second, still succeeded at keeping in his half-opened drawer the book he wanted to peruse, and notebooks tucked away under old waste papers. Having learned how to isolate himself from the noise of this large, sonorous, multi-floored room, he pursued his work.

But, as everything comes out into the open sooner or later, the supervisors learned through anonymous informants of the mysterious occupations of Le Loup and increased his load of work. And yet, right to the end, his desk would hide a text; and thin sheets of paper (cut precisely to the size of the width of the columns of the register!)

would fill up with the expected articles. Thus were started a few translations from English of Jane Leade, Prentice Mulford, and William Law. Later, following the traditions of any venerable elder of a Lodge who respects himself and follows traditions, Sédir decided to present a thesis upon Jacob Boehme, a great figure of the past, the "Most Beloved Master," as Louise-Claude de Saint-Martin had called him.

First, a small brochure on the life of the shoemaker-philosopher came out at Chamuel (with a pen-sketch portrait by Sédir himself). Then he undertook the quite formidable translation of *De Signatura Rerum*, which Paul Chacornac was to publish seven years later. To translate this dense, sixteenth-century German (still more obscure because it emanated from an uneducated man), to transcribe its system, with all its subtle and hidden keys, required not only total mastery of the language but also patience and astounding comprehension. Being undertaken amid a thousand activities, this work is the forerunner of the program Sédir took upon himself later, when he will write: "One of the sacred texts upon which Jacob Boehme meditated the most was 'The Father who is in heaven will send the Holy Spirit to whomever asks it of him.'"

Another brochure that came out at this time, titled *The Creation*, avows his further detachment from the doctrines of the Brahmanic Vedanta.

In any event, an orientation toward Christian Hermeticism had already been outlined by Hoene-Wronski, and especially by the Marquis de Saint-Yves d'Alveydre, whose various books entitled "Missions…"[13] rallied a great many

---

[13] *La Mission des Français, La Mission des Juifs, La Mission des Ouvriers—Application sociale de la Synarchie, La Mission des Souverains.*

followers; and although living in seclusion, the author welcomed truly interested seekers. Sédir was among them. Living alone in his grand Versailles mansion, the courteous old gentleman (under the inspiration of his wife, who had died shortly before) was pursuing what he considered to be a synthesis of all sciences, the arcana of the West, the famous *Archeomètre,* which the whole of the wide world of seekers awaited.[14]

More theoretical than practical, this imposing system had the exceeding advantage of demonstrating that the gospel, more than any other sacred book (because of the divine presence of Christ) contains all the truth—the *Pater Noster* (Lord's Prayer) being its key.

Papus, in one of his works, evokes the old Marquis, and draws a parallel between the two masters living in France. But Sédir had already made his choice.

From the social standpoint, the activity of the Hermetic School had lately suffered a setback, a grave financial crisis due to the collapse of an attempt made in the U.S. by a certain Mr Bliss who had founded Lodges and had taken on the task of helping the Paris movement. Chamuel, not being able to subsidize it by himself, had to back out for a while. In spite of the creation of a third lodge, one had still to subsist within the means actually at hand.

None of these things preoccupied Sédir for any length of time, so certain was he that all organizations are ephemeral, that each esoteric system reaches a superior result, and that

---

[14] The voluminous work was not published until much later. Financial difficulties obliged Papus to organize the "Society of the Friends of Saint-Yves d'Alveydre," which permitted the publication of this first edition.

any religion contains within itself a mysticism that surpasses it. Only the doctrine of the first Rosicrucians, and the work of a few isolated great mystics, still attracted him.

In order to make contact with the one whom he had perceived as a "good family man," Sédir spent his vacation of August 1898 at Lyon. And though we know nothing about this "secret garden," it seems possible to tie it in to a few conversations Sédir will include later in his biographical work *Initiations*, and in particular with the character of the "Doctor," who incarnates the man of science in the occult domain, the initiate who rushes in all good faith to storm truth, only to find on all sides the inexorable barrier that throws him back toward the "usual tumult"—only to hear Andreas telling him: "Yes, there is a wall." "Is this wall temporary?" asks the troubled soul. "Should I climb over it or destroy it? Is it I who built it in the past? Is it an adversary? Is it a friend?"—"I cannot tell you, Doctor," says Andreas, "you must see for yourself; you can destroy this wall, go around it, climb over it, or dig beneath it; but don't try anything yet. Wait."

And so, though the groping period of feeling his way had passed, Sédir will obediently wait a few more years for the order to act: to receive his mission.

⊕

Up to this period in Sédir's life, his studies, incessant writings, and increasing stature in the spiritual movements of the time had removed any matrimonial ideas from his mind. He was aware of the combats and also of the power of a chaste life, and although his role as educator had attracted a great many female admirers, he had kept his distance. Not wanting to exalt the man we have been scruti nizing through any idolatrous bias, we can affirm that regardless of any gossips and critiques in this domain, they were always founded upon mere appearances, and are hence worthless.

In spite of the mystical asceticism to which Sédir adhered his whole life long, it was in Lyon that the idea of establishing a home took hold. A home, or marriage, is something one cannot undertake, or be liberated from, without facing compromises. The absolute point of view in marriage means that through pre-established choice the spouses become a team, walk together toward God, undertake getting along together and modifying each other daily.

Sédir's first spouse was beyond question an exemplary one, and her death worthy of a saint's. As with many other Parisian workers, Alice Perret-Gentil applied her needleworking skills in her employment as a dressmaker, but was obliged to augment her meager salary by sewing at home. It was in this manner, while working for Mme Encausse, that she met Sédir. But there was such a financial impediment! His salary at the bank did not surpass 3,000 francs per year; as yet, his published works brought in nothing. But even so, without a thought of the morrow, they married on June 13, 1899.

A few friends who attended both the civil and religious consecrations partook of a simple meal at the old Café Voltaire. Present were Papus and Chamuel, who had stood as witnesses, also the journalist Serge Basset (later killed at the outset of the World War), and a few old occultists who came to cheer on the newly-weds. Thanks to the friendship of a young artist, the young couple, now obliged to vacate the mansard room of the Avenue de l'Opéra, took an apartment at 3 rue d'Orchampt, near to summit of Montmartre.

A short time later, Mme Le Loup found a small apartment 500 feet away, at 14 rue Girardon, where they all spent ten relatively happy and calm years.

We find these happy years and the ensuing pattern of this change in their lives reflected in a few lovely pages from *Initiations*: for example, where are described the plateaus of Vélizy and the Compiegne Forest, which evoke the lovely foliage of the Île-de-France, where the young couple would pass their Sundays entertained by friends. And when summer came, they in turn would entertain at Neuilly, in the tolerably spacious villa that an admirer loaned them each year. They would play charades, wear disguises, dance, play ball or quoits.

These noisy recreational meetings, however, did not in any sense modify the spiritual program then more and more taking shape. This home atmosphere even enabled Sédir to better fulfill his bank employment. Arriving at rue Ventadour at 10 a.m., he could, due to his working facility, accomplish his task in one straight stretch and then have the whole lunch hour to write, or else to rectify the errors of an unskilled colleague.

For her part, Mme Le Loup, outside of her household duties, did not remain inactive. She would copy articles or manuscripts, visit the sick, and often undertake research at the Bibliothèque Nationale (though that particular chore was soon given over to an elderly unemployed family man, which, given charitably for a long period of time, rather depleted the young couple's budget). As far as new publications were concerned, as we have mentioned, they became limited since Chamuel had had to step back. In 1901, Ollendorff published Sédir's *Elements of Hebrew*, and *The Magic Letters*. Two years later, a bibliography of studies on the Rosicrucians and the preface to the treatise on *The Revolution of Souls* by Isaac Luria came out.

But then, Sédir, having met Médéric Beaudelot through friends, found an most understanding and faithful publisher. Beaudelot was one of the most attractive personalities of the times. A fervent follower of Allan Kardec and Léon Denis, he began by publishing a spiritualistic paper that, after meeting Sédir, would in time become the journal *Psyché*, to which Sédir contributed articles for a long time.

This vibrant man incarnated the prototype of the knight in search of an ideal. Always ready to help, he would receive anyone in a somber, meager ground floor apartment (which was referred to as a bookstore) on the rue du Bac. A hall next door became the meeting-place of the new Lodge known as the "Sphinx." Living at Bourg-la-Reine at the same time as Péguy and Léon Bloy, Sédir's house became the rendezvous of the first "Friends."[15] One usually played ball, and so it came about one day that Sédir stumbled against the root of a tree, provoking a grave complication to the side of his leg, which developed into a tumor that cost him part of his mobility.

Meanwhile, the Hermetic School followed its usual curriculum. Respecting the personality and concepts of those involved, Sédir would never have thought of criticizing anyone on account of his own shifting viewpoint. But one evening at the end of the trimester, after he had delivered his class on astrology and magic, the public was astonished to discover that the program for the coming months included

---

[15] That is, those who over time formed the association *Les Amitiés Spirituelles* (Friends in Spirit) around Sédir and his work. This association still exists.

no esoteric subjects, but instead a series of lectures on the New Testament!

From that day on, Sédir never mounted the podium but for the sole goal of developing this new orientation of his thought—before a smaller audience now, but one that never forsook him. For three quarters of an hour, commencing at 9 p.m, he would develop (in a subdued, monotone voice) the themes that would later be called "his doctrine." At the close, he would answer questions that had been written in advance and left on the table.

This life, which as we have noted began in mediocrity and suffering, due to the wealth of his exceptional gifts, may well have taken a triumphant turn, as so many do. The depth of knowledge and the authority with which Sédir was endowed added to the rapidity of his comprehension in all domains. Moreover, the beauty and clarity of his style could have opened wide either a singularly renowned literary or philosophical career! But before each new bifurcation destiny offers us, before each more or less fortunate solicitation, the choice of one who deliberately abandons speculative values in order to consecrate himself to the one master of eternity is always to intentionally choose the place, the position, or the assignment least representative of his gifts, or the most thankless!

This is what unconscionable critics—those who remain in the no-man's-lands searching for the masters of the earth—will call a "failed mysticism."

⊕

Beyond what we can perceive of someone as regards their impact or their profound role, simply taking into consideration the human refractions that a divine determinism has marked differently (and even those are being influenced by a secondary atmosphere and ethnic currents), we finally face here a complex and almost indecipherable morphology.

The secret march of evolution also involves a variety of itineraries, depending on the individual—exalting some, reducing others, without, however, it being possible to judge any of them. Some, taking the steepest paths, take on a special radiance in the eyes of those on the plains. Their position on the plateau then seems inaccessible to us. Having so expeditiously reached the altitude that his eagle-eyes permitted him, Sédir, as we have already seen, was one of those. But the originality of his case was that he did it while modifying his whole personality. In fact, in the eyes of all who knew him, his bearing, his speech, his whole being gradually changed.

However, someone close to him became a heavy load to bear in this second period of his life—a dolorous load indeed (whom many might have reproached him for, socially speaking), but who nevertheless contributed to the path of sacrifice Sédir had accepted, requiring him to acquire all the qualities of the spiritual leader that he was. (But one had to be closely entwined in this drama to understand the heroism entailed in this.)

Counter to those thought of as initiates, whom some call "masters," and who for a while exert upon their disciples an excessive authority, an ephemeral prestige, he, to the contrary, will always remain profoundly humble in his role of self-effacement toward his friends. Rather, he sought to lessen his powers, his incontestable means, by placing himself on the level of those he directed.

In reality, never did his tastes change. Craving solitude, a shepherd's hut in the mountains, he willingly transforms his habits and tendencies in view of touching the greatest number of people.

Drawn to the humble people, the masses whose generous riches he appreciated, loving both children and animals, right after the death of his wife Alice he took a stand and settled among the bourgeois world, the snobs. Overcoming his timidity and (though it cost him much) without thought of the morrow (since he no longer had any encumbrances), he left the Banque de France, and with his future assured, left Montmartre and moved successively first to the rue de Beaune, then rue Cardinet, and finally rue de Seine. His door was open day and night to all who wanted to see him; his home, with esthetically choice, yet simple, furnishings, welcomed everyone.

He, whose tendency was rather bohemian, even untidy, who took no notice of his clothes except that his wife saw to it, all of a sudden learned how to wear a collar (and they were very high at that time), to select his ties, to take care of his hands. He parted his rebellious locks of hair in the center, well-combed. To meet social invitations, in the evening he wore the prescribed full-dress and chose raglan coats in order to hide the gimp of his leg.

His figure, previously thin, gauche, even sickly, became transformed due to the progressive training of physical culture he took and excelled in. This became a discipline he followed in spite of fevers and fatigues to such a degree that, without exaggerating, he could claim to "do anything I want with my body."

Soon the large frame he had inherited from the Rhenish ancestry of his mother filled out. His rather thick neck gave him both an imposing stature and an easy deportment.

Though he scrupulously weighed how he spent his time,

he began visiting art galleries, and kept in touch with new literary works. Always encumbered with a four-footed friend, for which he cared paternally, and in spite of the affection those lovely animals gave back to him, it complicated his life constantly. He had a particular interest in the Brie species, and a whole dynasty of dogs of various sizes and awkward progeny, many of whom bore the name of Guérotte, accompanied him in life.

Having become a member of the Club des Briards, he wrote a book upon the breeding of these animals, possessed of such extraordinary intelligence and devotion. A few moving pages relating examples of what these dogs can furnish humans are to be found in his works.

These transformations confounded many earlier friends, who could not quite understand these changes, and were therefore quite affected; a few young neophytes, arriving full of zeal with their uncompromising "natural" or vegetarian principles, could not quite accept the man, surprised at finding a well-dressed, meticulous, almost elegant mystic, whereas, in fact, renunciation of earthly values was at the core of his teaching.

Yet, all along the centuries have there not been many such confounding examples—for instance, the well-known figure of Cagliostro? Bearing the imprint of exceptional power, such men mystify history in spite of historian-biographers trying to pigeonhole them as adventurers or impostors—so difficult is it to detect the role true servants of God have come to perform, while seemingly being "friends of unwarranted wealth."

Did not Jesus two thousand years ago scandalize the doctors of the law, the Pharisees, and even his close associates?

As everything is bound together, the outer transformation of Sédir did nothing but refract the very much more important transformation of his inner life and his radiation! While at the very beginning of his mission he had affected anonymity in the teaching he gave regarding the various viewpoints of the spirit, suddenly, without warning, without pressuring anyone, he asserted a doctrine that he professed to be a precise personal path, all the while continuing to lecture and answer questions from the floor.

This change of attitude, while imposing a larger field of action and a chance of circulating more and more, enabled him to meet, in the most diverse domains, the more influential personalities of the day, and, more especially, to reach numerous souls in distress.

Only the framework changed, because his faithful followers—who had heard him develop theories of occultism at Chamuel's, at a café on the Place de l'Odéon, on the ground floor rue de Savoie, at "Père Chocolat" on rue de la Harpe (where one partook of the beverage after the meetings), in the rear courtyard of the rue du Bac near the Beaudelot bookshop, at the Hermetic School in two old buildings of the rue Séguier—trustful of his word, followed the new expositions he gave of the gospels in the hall rue Cardinet, where the regular talks took place at first; then, during the World War, at the Sociétés Savantes; and later, with an ever growing public, in the large hall of the Société pour l'Encouragement de l'Industrie rationale across from Saint-Germain-des-Prés. Out of town and in foreign countries, his friends organized for him series of lectures. Also, the various Universités Populaires (very much in vogue for the study of disparate subjects) invited him for the first time in 1913 in a hall of the Faubourg Saint-Antoine, then in 1925 before a less democratic public in a hall of boulevard

Raspail, headquarters of the Université Mercereau. This turned out to be the last time Sédir spoke in public.

⊕

Humanly speaking, Sédir's ambition (and he certainly had some) could not be limited to the domain of intellect or of knowledge, still less to that of power. Having tested the weaknesses and feverishness of these values, and in spite of the respect he accorded them, neither would he waste his time with, still less exploit, them. Service toward a high ideal had drawn him ever since a very youthful age, and this ideal, having become more explicit in the revelation of Christ as the sole aim, the goal of his life—he had thus become committed… Howsoever, this Master who had chosen him, as he does for each of his servants throughout eternity, once more put his trust in him and gave him definite directives. The order was: "You will write and you will speak up to the day when no one shows up anymore." And so, Sédir kept on writing, lecturing everywhere he was asked—finally understanding, after profound studies, that the gospels, emanating directly out of the Book of Life, are the exact refraction of the passage of the Word upon the earth.

However, as they are transposable *ad infinitum* even as to their "letter" (and since theologies and doctrines become confounded), these four little books need interpreters attuned to their respective epochs.

Speaking to other persons during those same years, that "authorized" person[16] had also said that "the gospels would

---

[16] A reference to Maître Phillipe, of whose role in Sédir's life more will be said.

be rewritten" (which confirms the role Sédir was to play in our twentieth century). Up to that time, his articles, his writing, had been limited to the closed field of Hermeticism, but they had been so numerous and of such superior quality as to launch his name and to win him a preponderant place in the company of searchers. Although his tendency towards and awakening to Christian mysticism was considered a "desertion" by many, still, they continued to read and listen to him.

As with any profound work, Sédir's was decanted slowly and purified itself. In the first of those of his works[17] published by Beaudelot between 1907 and 1911, one still finds, along with his new inspiration, vestiges of occult phraseology, symbolism, and a few Eastern correspondences. These disappeared in revisions of the two volumes that eventually became *The Childhood of Jesus* (which came out on the eve of the First World War) and *The Sermon on the Mount.*[18] To that end, integrated citations from the four gospels were included at the beginning of each chapter. "That will force them to read," said Sédir—thinking of the many seekers who did not know or did not read the gospel texts anymore.

Shortly thereafter, *Mystic Forces and the Conduct of Life* came out in twelve short brochures. They were compiled from a series of lectures given at rue Séguier, and to another

---

[17] In 1912, *The Spiritual Duty* was published by request of those who then called themselves his students, and who sought precise directives. A later edition was retitled *The Spiritual Path.*

[18] Our friend Albert Legrand, who had taken charge of the works of Sédir, published *The Sermon on the Mount* at Bihorel-les-Rouen in 1921. Then came *The Healings of Christ, The Kingdom Of God,* and *The Crowning of His Work,* which constitute all Sédir has set down in writing on the gospels.

group in Nice. Donors enabled the publication of these various books and brochures.

Finally, the building where Sédir lived on rue de Seine became a meeting place. It was there that he wrote the brochure *The Seven Mystical Gardens*, which in a very few pages offers a startling description of the various steps leading to eternal landscapes, of a quality on a par with those of St Teresa of Avila, St John of the Cross, and other dwellers on the summits.

*Initiations*, however, is the book that was most appreciated, and that also passed through the most transformations. Written practically in one stroke in a small garden of Bourg-la-Reine, at the verge of his illumination, it was published in small format in 1908 by Beaudelot. But this little brochure was too incendiary, too overwhelming a subject to leave it there; being the crossroads and program of an entire life, it needed to be developed, and above all transposed to the different planes of evolution—in fact to the many grades where we, schoolchildren that we are, pass and pass again.

Sédir, reprising his favorite subject, gave it a vaster field. The short story turned into a powerful book in which the iridescence of human thought in its social and metaphysical concepts, and even in its religious forms, discreetly restored Christ and his doctrine to their rightful place. The second edition of *Initiations* came out in 1917, with the subtitle "A Story for Little Children." Yes! And how! And with the dedication: "To my friends, to thank them for their eager longing toward the one Shepherd whose love gathers our dispersions and brings us back to the Father's house."

This edition quickly sold out. The theme was then taken up again, new chapters were added, and at the end of the

First World War, the third and final edition came out.[19] Two important new chapters had been added, with facts and anecdotes relative to the constant presence of the Master. It must be confessed, however, that Sédir was not happy with this third edition. Although grateful to have it, we can nonetheless understand his reservations, owing to his innate desire for perfection. On the other hand, he was under the impression that the cinema might have been a better medium to express the atmosphere, both simple and miraculous, that pervades the book. To our mind, it is just as well that film editors did not take it up.

In our feverish age of social machinations and complexities, the great originality of this work was to revive a living image of Christ. Sédir was the first to bring Christ as a living presence to the humble people, to the sick—to put him, one could say, on the street among us. Later, in various ways, other writers followed suit.

In the domain of praxis, Sédir had already formed a group of men of goodwill whom he coached toward profound, serious action. Then, right after the First World War, when he had organized and revived the movement to a higher level, a new role developed in Sédir: the "schoolmaster," the soul director, began to emerge above and beyond the lecturer and writer.

All of us, enthusiastic followers filled with illusions, driven by our legitimate desire to serve actively, urged Sédir to launch a publication, a review that would be a means of broadcasting, and especially of becoming a link with our sympathizers in the provinces. Ever since his debut with

---

[19] In 1982, long after this present biography was written, some additional chapters were added to a fourth edition.

Chamuel, Sédir (having always been submerged in the inherent difficulties of periodicals) understood the need for such diffusion, and so he accepted; and in true Sédirian fashion, assumed all responsibilities for this publication—a burden that cost him many a sleepless night.

The first issue came out February 1919. The subscription was for a year, at five francs (happy days!) and the bulletin came out monthly. The first number proclaimed: "There must be a few amateurs of the impossible."

Then came the consecration. In the July 16, 1920 issue of the *Journal Official* appeared the announcement of a "free, benevolent, charitable Christian Association called *Les Amitiés Spirituelles*, whose doctrine and purpose—to serve Christ as "the only master"—were nothing new, at least nothing that came from the mind of a man, or from one of those ephemeral concepts, such as the nineteenth century saw emerge under the various names known to religious history.

In reality, it was nothing other than a continuation of the small phalanxes that from St John and St Paul (to mention only the earliest apostles) try to preserve the integrity of gospel mysticism, and work for a heavenly Jerusalem still far away—for a kingdom beyond time that brings together true Friends. Its founder, refusing and disdaining illusory successes, was aware that the ascent is steep, that quantity and quality must never be confused, and that the letter must never be taken for the spirit.

Sédir was in full form, at his best. Yet he was going to leave us… And we, unaware of this, were demanding more and more from him!

To his presentations on mysticism came further works: *A Few Friends of God* and short pieces entitled "Ascetic

Energy," "The Gospel and Sapience," "Love your Neighbor." Moreover, as we friends were insistent on a laïc breviary, he put together for us the truly magnificent *Fifty-Two Weekly Meditations*. Then came "The Education of the Will" and "The Three Sacrifices," which were published posthumously.[20]

⊕

Jan Bielecki, one of our most ardent friends in the service of Christ, had just passed away in the early part of January 1926. Referring to his passing, Sédir had written: "I ask you to recall to mind unceasingly the example of Bielecki, true ascetic of knowledge and of charity. When heaven deprives us of a visible guide, let us not neglect to make an *examen* and ask ourselves if we have taken into account how to profit from all the resources and instructions this guide offered us." Little did we know that a few weeks later, these words would hold the same imperative duty for our whole association.

His intimate friends had noticed a certain slackening in the severe discipline of the athlete; having had to abandon his apartment, rue de Seine, due to distressing circumstances, ever since his return from vacation Sédir was living with friends on the second floor of their private home, rue Henri-Heine, in Passy.[21] They had allotted him a bedroom and a library where he could continue his arduous task. In that well-organized brain, creative work never stopped; his

---

[20] Later, we were able to launch the last unpublished works of Sédir: *History and Doctrine of the Rosicrucians*, *Christian Mysticism*, and *The Incandescent Path*.

[21] Mme de Graffenried, daughter of the explorer, Marquis de Mores.

moving Appeal for France had just been launched; three lectures had been announced to be given in February on: "The Sacrifice in Antiquity," The Sacrifice of Jesus Christ," and "The Sacrifice of the Disciple."[22] This program, which never took place, was made the more concrete by his own sacrifice.

His whole being had been showing great fatigue—a few words of lassitude, a slackening in his occupations, a persistent cold, constant headaches that obliged him to press a large boil near his nose, from which black blood exuded— all of which denoted a congestive state and abnormal depression. But we were so accustomed to seeing him outgoing, affectionate, and concerned with our difficulties, that we selfishly did not attach much importance to these symptoms, which only later became classified in our minds.

In these winter months of 1925 we were particularly happy to have him among us more often, since, when not in town, he would attend our Friday meetings regularly.

On January 15, 1926, leaving our hall, rue de Seine, we walked with him up to the place of the Théatre-Français. Continuing our discussion, we went for a glass of beer. As the "Poverello" used to say regarding the talks he had with his young Brothers, Sédir too would "let himself be fleeced" while caressing his dog or giving her food. But that evening, feeling a chill, he took a taxi and went home earlier than usual.

A week later, our reunion missed the absent "boss." Then, on Monday morning the 25th, one of our closest friends, entering Sédir's bedroom, sensed that something unusual had happened. Nothing had been moved, yet an

---

[22] Published by Albert Legrand in 1926.

atmosphere of drama reigned. The sole witness of that night had been Sédir's dog Guérotte, who, in a fright, threw herself at the visitor, then went to lie by the bed of her master; she later had to be taken from the house.

Sédir was in a high fever and suffering from violent pains in his head. A doctor was summoned and diagnosed general septicemia. Excepting the three close friends attending him, no one was allowed into his room. Felled by a high fever, barely able to speak, he still manifested his pleasure at seeing us. News of his illness spread; consternation reigned, each person wanting to participate at nursing; letters and advice poured in. But to all these affectionate offers, his sense of obedience and example, which he had himself prescribed as necessary to follow through the normal course of events, made him decline anything not prescribed by the doctor. He knew only too well, and had often written, that providence decides and directs all things under the most banal of appearances. The affluence and lifestyle of his hosts permitted him nursing around the clock, and when typhoid became certain (the second blood tests having revealed the source of illness), the library next to his bedroom was rapidly transformed into a room for convalescence.

All in all, within the fold of Les Amitiés Spirituelles, optimism reigned. Despite the prevailing sadness and ardent prayers that friends recited even below his windows and in the four corners of France, one accepted, one understood, the ordeal—but certainly never anticipated his death. At fifty-five, Sédir was in full form. He could not leave us! It was unthinkable; we needed him badly!

Alas, one could see that he was weakening from day to day. The following Friday it was apparent that he was failing. The medical staff began to worry about the state of his heart.

In the beginning, when not yet knowing the cause of the fever one was fighting, Sédir's aspect was one of agitation, of disorder. His eyes particularly were startling, because, due to his myopia, he ordinarily kept them half-closed; but now, in delirium, without seeing, they were opened wide upon hallucinatory images. His enormous dark pupils were constantly rotating in their deep-set and dark-brown orbits. His beard had grown, the half-open dried caked lips gave his face an expression of a man undergoing torture. Feverishness alternated with extreme agitation, which was then followed by a period of prostration with a return of lucidity with which one had to deal tactfully.

On Sunday, neither baths nor antithermics could check the rising temperature; the fragile, feeble heart had to be sustained. Heaven turned a deaf ear to our prayers; all hope seemed lost. Monday and Tuesday went by, but the lungs were filled, he was breathing oppressively; on Wednesday his power of resistance was exhausted. The hour had come!

During the morning our anxiety mounted as his strength visibly decreased; the phone rang ceaselessly. The hosts and two friends were seated in the living room when at four p.m. the nurse asked us to go upstairs—the end was near. The second-floor bedroom was more silent than ever. A presence hovered in the room; one felt the great messenger having come to accomplish her task. The half-closed window curtains let in a grayish light; the patient, in bed in the center of the room, propped up by pillows, still dominated the situation. Overcome by emotions, our four shadows glided into the room. Sédir, sensing our approach more than being able to see us, made a gesture with his left arm, on the window side, as if he wanted to draw us toward him. Madame de Graffenried came in tears, knelt by the foot of the bed, while his long, diaphanous hand caressed her head affectionately. Then, drawing her to him, he kissed her forehead; and her husband, who was sustaining her, also bent his face for a farewell kiss.

Not a word was said, neither could the dying man, who was beyond that possibility, nor the witnesses with a lump in their throats. Only the large white hand spoke in the silence. Then in a last gesture, his hand motioned for the two friends,[23] to come for the kiss of peace—the last. The image of Christ hanging in the empty alcove was presented to him, and in one long regard of adoration—symbol of his whole life—Sédir made his final effort... The head, which had been slightly raised, fell back, his breathing, slowing more and more, stopped definitively at 6:45 p.m.

That night, three friends kept watch over the one who had given them such profound joys. The bed had been repositioned in the alcove. Freshly shaven and washed, Sédir had almost regained his normal aspect. Death, however, had etched his features: from the very pure line of the forehead followed the profile of a nose more aquiline than it had been in life. The mouth, rather like that of Pascal through its almost dolorous fold, neutralized an unexpectedly strong, deeply-hewn mask, reminiscent of the Corsair ancestor who probably had deeded him a few traits—reflec-

---

[23] The two friends at his bedside were Emile Besson (1885–1975) and the author of this article, Max Camis (1890–1985). The memoir following the present one in this book is from the pen of Emile Besson. Because of the intimacy of these two friends with Sédir, Besson's memoir will be given in full, even though, of course, similar ground will be covered. Each memoir has its special nuance.

tor of one aspect of the hardy and proud character with which he had to battle his whole life.

As for the feelings of those who kept watch by the long, still body, beyond the pain they all felt, and the confusion at the loss of their chief, there followed a calm, almost happy, impression of peace. The distress, the anguish, of the past days, the restraint of the invisible presence of the genii of death that had come to fulfill the order of the sealed letter each of us brings along at birth—all of that gave place to the certitude that all this was but appearance, not reality. The beloved guide that heaven had placed upon our path remained. This impression lasted during the three nights of the watch, when other friends took turns at their posts by the two flickering flames of the candelabra and the bouquet of Parma violets by the bedside.

How many happy memories and animated conversations were evoked during these nights abumbrated by a winged presence!

Then came the funeral, the religious service at the Church of Notre-Dame de la Miséricorde, all of it too ostentatious for the taste of many, but which was the manifestation of a well-to-do family who saw in Sédir someone greater than a family member.

His body was buried in the little St Vincent Cemetery, a few feet away from the rue Girardon, close to the tomb of his first wife Alice Le Loup. What remained of our guide was then deposited, in thin poplar planks, into the earth.

We were all amazed that not a trace, not a note, not an order, nor special directives were to be found among his papers; no choice as to who should be the one to replace him—who could have replaced him anyway? Not a letter to the directors he had chosen. Nothing—nothing but the simple retirement, obliteration, of the servant who, once his task is finished, abandons—as his Master had done on the Cross—everything into the hands of the Father.

But for us, his work is still there, filled with a program, as he himself told us, "for many lives to come." There is nothing to do but continue, alone now, and yet with, by, and for Christ.

Left to right: Dr. Gerard Encausee (Papus); Dr. Emmanuel Lalande (Marc Haven); Nizier Anthelme Philippe (Maître Philippe); Yvon Le Loup (Paul Sédir)

# Paul Sédir:

## by *Émile Besson*

n February 3 1926, in Paris, one of the most prestigious and moving voices ever heard was silenced—a voice that had poured consolation, certitude, and peace into the hearts of many people—the voice of Paul Sédir.

"A voice" said the poet Théophile Briant, "that had consecrated itself to the diffusion of the gospels for years, and that had warned us against the multiplied prostitutions of Christ's Word."

"The debt of our times," said Sédir, "will be heavy when so much unhealthy prose is printed, when so many nefarious and empty words are hurled from pulpit and rostrum."

"Silence" he wrote in 1923, "is not the unspoken word or non-speaking; it is a positive act, an affirmative force; it is a genie, it is a god. It is a hidden kingdom, and it progresses, as do all other creatures, between two counselors: an angel of light and an angel of darkness.

"Everything speaks in the universe; but also, everything listens. Usually one seeks to find out what creatures are saying, but sages are more concerned with finding out what they pass over in silence.

"If the world of sounds contains the intellectual nourishment of our spirit, the world of silence is that of mystery, the place where ideals are held in reserve, the original kingdom of truth, of beauty and of goodness. Its doors are narrow and one finds them only after having wandered a long while among the brambles of speech. One must have experienced the truth of the Persian poem: 'The word you hold back is your slave; the one that escapes you is your master.' Who can foresee the consequences of a word? Speech between two silences is similar to time between two eternities, or space between two infinites. To speak is to sow; but it is in the silence that mysteries are celebrated and gods plough souls."

Paul Sédir, whose real name was Yvon Le Loup, was born January 2, 1871, at rue de Lainerie, in Dinan, France. He was the son of Hippolyte Le Loup and Séraphine Foeller, his wife, from Neustadt, near Fulda (Hesse-Nassau).

He did not remain long in his native Brittany, but spent most of his childhood in Paris, first in the Batignolles section, then at 4 Avenue de l'Opéra. The one writing these lines lived for twenty years close to him, and for the last twelve of these years in daily contact as an intimate friend. He can vouch that the life of Sédir was one of humility and self-effacement.[1]

Let us immediately state that what drew so many of us to him, what made us cling to him, was most assuredly the scope of his mind, the nobility of his sentiments, his affability and grace, his radiation; but above all, his sincerity. Sédir lived what he preached, in profound simplicity; he was a living example of the virtues he extolled, bringing the luminosity they contained to the attention of his listeners and readers. In him, words and actions formed a magnificent unity. He was, in all the truth and grandeur of the expression, a servant of Christ.

[1] Emile Besson, 1885–1975 (see note 23, page 44).

That is why his words had such resonance. A simple word from his lips would move us, would stir us to our very depths, because it was a cataract gushing from his heart, the expression of a spiritual reality not only understood but lived. Near him one felt secure spiritually, one felt oneself to be a better person; everything became clear and simple; we would be incited to work with courage, to endure, and go forth.

⊕

Possessing a prodigious memory, an extraordinary capacity for work, a keen analytical mind, and rare intuition, Sédir read and assimilated a considerable number of works—mostly those dealing with philosophy, symbolism, esotericism—while he subjected himself to veritable feats in order to create a literary style for himself. We believe there are no readers of Sédir's works who have not been captivated by the magnificence of his style. Above all, when he became aware that he was the bearer of a message of sublime importance, he wanted the form of this account to be as worthy as possible of the communication he had to transmit; and in truth, Sédir's style breathes a particular loftiness. Moreover, he speaks to the heart; he awakens in his reader a desire for the highest, for the best that slumbers in the depths of a being. He shows the path to the ideal, that austere but alluring path taken by the privileged beings Christ has designated as "the salt of the earth" and "the light of the world."

⊕

On June 13, 1899, Sédir married Alice Estelle Perret-Gentil, born September 5, 1867 near La Chaux-de-Fonds. She was for him a perfect mate and companion, an exemplary wife, a light who voluntarily kept in the background. She passed away ten years later. The year preceding her death (which was a saintly one) Sédir dedicated the second volume of his *Conférences sur l'Évangile*:

> To my beloved wife,
> To my silent collaboratrix,
> To the great heart who never feared to shoulder all suffering so that the words of the Master may here be clothed in a less imperfect form,
> I offer this book.
> From her came all that it contains of persuasiveness, from me all its shortcomings.

Sédir found happiness and joy in sharing the conquests of his mind with others. Each newly discovered horizon, each elucidated problem he passed on to those who, like him, were studying these venerable traditions.

He would receive his friends regularly on friday nights in his Montmartre apartment. The smallish dining room was overcrowded with a heterogeneous group of enthusiastic young people who, while drinking tea or coffee, would discuss sciences, esotericism, and magnetism, but who also smoked so much that the air was blue even on summer nights when the window was wide open. Whenever someone entered, Sédir would get up, shake hands over the heads, trying to find another seat if possible. Alice Sédir would zigzag among the various groups to serve the newcomer, and after the commotion of the new arrival and greetings had subsided, each one, drawn to a certain group by affinity, would resume the thread of conversation.

Though he was unpretentious, Sédir never could appear banal. He was a strange man who emanated a powerful radiation. He was the carrier of an interior light that would enlighten all who confided in him.

The host in those days had his oldest friends around him, dear faces most of whom are no longer with us, friends of the wonderful days of once-upon-a-time, who are now phantoms in our memories, but lamps upon our paths.

⊕

As Théophile Briant says again: "Sédir was to the esoteric sciences what Stéphane Mallarmé was to poetry." Of an encyclopedic culture, endowed with a prodigious power for work, he had encompassed and probed human knowledge, had explored all disciplines. He could discuss with equal mastery any possible subject. At the meetings in his home one could ask him questions, which he answered with the good graces that never left him. He would correct in precise sentences some of the ideas launched, or use a clever aside in which each of us could find a new lesson.

How many memories are re-awakened in our hearts as we turn our thoughts back to those days of the past! We will only relate three—we thus limit ourselves!

Two of his friends had embarked upon a probing philosophical discussion, the subject of which is of no consequence here. Each holding to his opinion, they could not get together nor agree. One of them exclaimed, "Let's go find Sédir, he will either cast a vote or conciliate our two points of view—and hey presto! no sooner said than done. If I remember rightly, it was then the middle of the night when they arrived at Sédir's apartment, continuing to argue before their indulgent mentor. He, dubitative, thoughtful, smiles, listens, shakes his head while puffing abundant swirls of smoke from his pipe, neither approving nor disapproving, saying never a word. But the two friends are delighted. All differences are overcome, they are in full accord. Of a sudden, the solution to the problem seems to be startlingly one of common sense and simplicity. Only later will they will recall that Sédir had not said a word.

Another aspect of Sédir's character was his faithfulness to duty. On a certain winter evening snow began falling in such abundance that in a few short moments all means of transportation were bought to a halt. One must admit it was the "happy epoch" before the advent of the subways. But it also happened to be one of his lecture nights. Many people would have thought it needless to bother putting themselves out, because it is a long way from Montmartre to the rue Séguier; many would have rationalized that the hall would be deserted and the trip to no purpose. But Sédir was not one of those. At the appointed hour he entered the small conference room where two ladies, who had equally braved the elements, were to be his only audience. Not the least fazed, as though the hall were filled, Sédir began his discourse before his two auditresses without abridging one word. Then he left at approximately ten o'clock, as if the weather were mild and serene—his duty accomplished.

Here is another of his actions showing to what extent his conduct was in perfect concordance with his convictions and his teaching.

One day, as he was leaving home, a man on the street accosted him, saying: "You do not know me, but I know you," and proceeded to tell him that if on that very day he could not find 40 francs (and these were gold francs), he would be evicted from his lodging—he, his wife, and his children. Sédir took a piece of paper out of his pocket, upon which he wrote: "Dear Alice, would you please give the bearer of this note 40 francs." He could have stated "precisely" 40 francs, because that was all that was in the house. Assuredly, it is not Sédir who let this be known. It was his dear Alice who told a few friends, adding: "Sédir understood it was God who had sent this man, because he had asked neither 35 francs, nor 50 francs, but the 40 francs we possessed."

⊕

For the many years we knew Sédir, we had always noticed the great prudence he exercised when speaking of things relating to the invisible realm. He always said that he knew nothing personally, limiting himself to repeating things he had been told or that he had read in general, without being specific, such as: "There are some who say…"

Then, one day, brusquely, without transition, this prudent form ceased. To the questions we put to him, from that time on, he answered authoritatively and with a peremptory affirmation: "Such a thing is thus; such a thing takes place in such a way." After having spoken for years of "having heard it said," he suddenly spoke of "knowing."

This corresponds to the time when, having reached the summit of knowledge and powers, he abandoned his titles, threw overboard his "treasures of wisdom," and, rejecting any kind of initiation and all logosophy, separated himself from most of his traveling companions in order to consecrate himself entirely to the gospels.

This development surprised his oldest friends, several of whom never understood it. Assuredly, this change corresponded to what was most profound within Sédir. Proof of that change is found in the "Course on Mysticism" he taught in 1896 and published in *L'Initiation* in 1898 (which already contains the seeds of his subsequent works). But then an unforeseen, solemn, decisive event took place in his life, an event that made him aware of the emptiness of sciences and secret societies, and put him forever on the one path of the gospels. From then on he had but one doctrine: the love for one's fellowman that gives the key to the world; and but one aim: to seek the kingdom of God, knowing that "all else" would be added unto him.

⊕

Regarding the pivotal event in his life, Sédir has made definite and important declarations. First, in a letter addressed on October 15, 1910 to the *Echo du Merveilleux* (which was reproduced later), then in the foreword he wrote for his *The Childhood of Jesus*, the principal passages of which are:

> I have stated in the foreword of the first edition that the ideas I expounded were not my own. "The one who furnished them to me," I added, will forgive me if I have involuntarily distorted his light; the omissions and the errors are mine; to him must revert all the good that his teaching has given me, and that it will still produce in spite of the incompetence of the interpreter.
>
> I renew that declaration with all the power I possess, but I still will not designate the one to whom I owe everything. It might be construed and said that my silence is an adroit ingratitude; I accept that misconception. I will continue to keep silent, in order to preserve a great number of metaphysicians from spurious slanders, the results of which are redoubtable . . . in

order to shield the work of my master from premature publicity; [and] finally, to keep him from being held responsible for my errors.

Finally and above all, Sédir refers to him in a chapter in his book *A Few Friends of God,* entitled "An Unknown."[2] In the last few years, Alfred Haehl, who was a very dear friend of Sédir, spoke openly about "The Unknown": Monsieur Nizier Anthelme Philippe. Alfred Haehl lived several years in close contact with Monsieur Philippe and wrote a work upon his master. The authenticity of all the elements contained in this book makes it a document of inestimable worth.[3] There he recorded what he saw and heard, completing his documentation and citations with those of other witnesses, whose friend he had become.

⊕

Sédir thus had the privilege of meeting his ideal, not in the abstract world of ideas, not as a conquest of intelligence, but in a living person—with all the mysterious and august reality that a living person possesses of unfathomable depth, luminous gentleness, and invincible certitude.

It was on the platform of the Lyon railroad station in Paris on a Sunday of July 1897 that, brought along by Papus, Sédir met for the first time the man he names "Andréas" in his novel *Initiations.* This "Andréas" is the one Papus had denominated "father of the poor" in an article consecrated to his spiritual master.

The meeting was brief, because the train was ready to

---

[2] This chapter is included in the present book.

[3] *Vie et Paroles du Maître Philippe*; Dervy Livres, 1 rue de Savoie, Paris 75006, 1959.

leave, and Sédir was able to exchange only a few words with this man. But Sédir saw him many other times in Paris, and made several trips to him—either in Lyon, where, assisted by Jean Chapas, Monsieur Philippe would receive numerous afflicted people who were healed and comforted—or in his home at L'Arbrèsle, where his faithful disciples would congregate (besides Jean Chapas, there were Marc Haven,[4] Alfred Haehl, etc.).

In May 1905, Sédir, with his wife Alice Le Loup, again spent two days near the one who was everything to them. It was Alice who had expressed the desire to go there, knowing that the time she had to remain on earth was limited, because the disease she suffered from was incurable. However, she did not leave this earth until 1909. But it was to be their last visit: The master passed away August 2, 1905.

⊕

The long illness that carried away Sédir's beloved companion having necessitated calm and rest, it was at Bourg-la-Refine that the meetings of friends resumed. The friend who had sheltered the young couple lived at the end of a cul-de-sac, in a pavilion called "Solitude," not very far from the home of Médéric Beaudelot. Every Sunday the old tram car would bring from the Porte d'Orléans the same faithful friends, coming to spend the afternoon with the one they already considered to be their guide. It was under the shade of the trees of this verdant Parisian suburb that Sédir wrote the very first, small and so captivating edition of *Initiations*, which we have already referred to.

---

[4] Marc Haven, pseudonym for Dr Emmanuel Lalande, who married Maître Philippe's daughter Victoire.

## Paul Sédir: by Émile Besson

Some years later, Sédir enlarged his *Initiations* to make of it the large work as it stands today, which is really "the most precious stone of the brilliant diadem representing his works."[5] There Sédir relates in fiction-like form his meetings with the "The Unknown." Here we must state precisely that there is not a detail in this story which is not materially true—all of it is fact.

The characters in this book are the Doctor, Stella, and the two envoys from heaven whom it is their privilege to encounter, Andréas and Théophane, regarding whom Sédir has given the following precisions:

> Théophane represents an inner aspect of Andréas: the pure light of the eternal soul, whereas Andréas is the immortal spirit. The Doctor represents the conscious mentality. Stella represents intuition. Regarded objectively, these characters represent levels or functions in the army of light.

⊕

It was the death of Alice Le Loup on April 23, 1909 that precipitated the reorientation of Sédir's life toward apostleship. He left the Banque de France. His friends urged him at the time to became the leader of a spiritual movement, but Sédir was not by nature an organizer. One will search his works in vain for a doctrine, a systematic teaching. And it was the same with his "unorganized" life and activities: his sole intent was to obey life's circumstances, which he regarded as the instruments or channels of the Father's will.

---

[5] Willy Schrödter, *Paul Sédir—une biographie* (in German) in *Der Spiegel*, February 1939.

If he was asked to give lectures, he gave them. If he was pressed to publish his lectures, he published them. Finally, when asked to gather together and teach the many people of goodwill who had united around him, he did so, forming an association.

Shortly thereafter he rented (in the vicinity of the rooms he had occupied in the rue de Beaune and later the rue Cardinet) a small sculptor's studio at 32 rue Cardinet, which became the first home of *Les Amitiés Spirituelles*. It was very simply, almost sparingly, furnished, but nonetheless bore the imprint of an aesthetic touch that did not have the upper hand over Sédir, but that he always sought. The remarkable scope of his knowledge and profound learning, which he placed at the service of the gospel, rapidly brought to him a new public, and his core faithful followers soon exceeded the locale. And so, Sédir rented a hall in the Hotel des Sociétés Savantes, rue Danton, then another at the Société d'Encouragement pour l'Industrie nationale, across the street from the Church Saint-Germain-des-Prés. Some time later, a close friend (killed in the course of the World War), the secretary of the brothers Marius and Ary Leblond, obtained for Sédir the small apartment at 10 rue du Cardinal-Lemoine, where the review *La Vie* was published. This apartment became the second home of the *Les Amitiés Spirituelles*.

God alone knows the depths of Sédir's devotion to his friends. For years he led us by the hand, listening to our problems with never-failing patience, forgetting his own pains to relieve our sorrows. For years he taught, sustained, advised, and consoled us. For years we heard his energetic and kind voice, faithfully echoing Him who became flesh for the salvation of the world. For years he tilled—at the price of what efforts!—the barren soil of our hearts, ever striving to enable them to receive the seeds of eternal life. For years, he took upon himself our load, the burden of our preoccupations, and also of our infidelities. He was a disciple of Him who came not to be served, but to serve and to give his life. Moreover, Sédir wanted to transform his friends into apostles. Here is the motto he gave them for their apostolate: "It is not by presentations of our ideas that we want to convince others, but by the radiation of the flame with which they set us on fire." In other words: "Example is the most persuasive eloquence."

⊕

One of his last letters ends with the following words: "Accept all of my prayers. Think only of Christ. Speak of nothing but Christ. Work only for Christ. Serve the poor and the sick. All the rest is only curiosity."

These words we can consider the résumé of the directives, the parting recommendations, of the one who became, from the time of his "encounter" up to the end of his life, a witness of Christ, a messenger of the gospel. His life and teachings were testimony rendered to the certitude that had filled and illuminated his being. He might well have claimed as his the words of St Paul: "Paul, slave of Jesus Christ. It is not I who live, but Christ who lives in me. Christ is my life."

A lady who belonged to the upper crust of Protestant society once told us: "When Sédir speaks of Christ, he is here, he is present." That was the secret of his apostolate. He placed us in the presence of Christ. Through him, it was Christ who spoke to us, who taught us, who encouraged us, who lifted us up again.

Just as Christ filled all Sédir's thoughts, filled all his love, filled all his hopes, so was the gospel his whole faith, his whole proselytism. He would answer all our questions, dissipate all our worries, restore our confidence and hope, revivify our certitude, by the light of the gospel. The spirit permeates his books. The pages he wrote upon the gospels are among the most moving, most comforting, one can ever hope to read.

Yet he never wanted to hear of an austere Christianity. He often repeated the well-known words: "a sad saint is a sorry saint." He wrote to his friends:

> A profound and grave incomprehension regarding the gospel is to believe that, because it asks of us renunciation, it forbids us any joys. In this we are much mistaken. Yes, there is in fact nothing pure on earth, but the fault is ours, because even were perfect beauty offered us, we would never recognize its value. Since we are impure and unworthy, we reject it. And yet there palpitates within us still the memory of and hope for a homeland without frontiers that, far beyond the stars, unfolds its landscapes under ever-shining midday suns. We know a land of beatitude exists; we would like to drop anchor there, but we do it in a stiff and awkward way: we strive to adopt love's gestures, but with the surly expressions of the miser refractory to alms-giving; toward the clear skies through which float smiling angels we only lift our sullen faces.
>
> We must let go! God is not only in the infinite, He permeates the finite also; heaven does not exclude earth. If we want to draw others up there, why conceal that heaven is a benevolent place? Why not reveal that

its air is delightful to breathe? Yes, to wallow in the limited joys of the world is an error, but to loath any healthy mundane joys, which are the sole small beauties we are able to gather along these pathways, is another error besides. Burst into blossom! Open the doors and windows. Give a cheery welcome to any being or any thing. "Love ye one another" does not mean to impose upon one another annoyances, no matter how much or little we may dissimulate them. May your encounters be festive. Be the sunshine of one another. You may not be rich in money, but you can give lavishly from your heart.

⊕

Such is the ideal Sédir presented. Théophile Briant, who penetrated deeply into the thoughts, heart, and faith of Sédir, has written: "Sédir extends to us the torch he received from a mysterious hand; it is up to us to take hold of it, if we are worthy!" Then he adds:

> Even when plunged in deepest sorrow, we must never despair. The promise of the Lord is formal. God is always among us. He will be among us until the end of the world. But we must not seek Him on the stage or in palaces or in places where trumpets of renown are sounding. He, like Sédir's "Unknown," is lost among the anonymous crowd. He conceals Himself from the curiosity of the warped minds of the perverted ones.
>
> Let us love our brothers as ourselves and we will find Him […] He is probably among the poor, needless to say, for he would keep no fortune but the one the invisible Archangel who walks by His side dis-

penses to Him each day. He is among us. He keeps watch and awaits our coming. He carries, as did St Tarcisius,[6] the Eucharist of his heart among men, and he is the depository of the tongues of fire. Beneath his nondescript clothing he hides the splendor of Mt Tabor, and is assuredly the salvation of the world."

⊕

After severing his connection with the Institute founded by Papus, Sédir gave a series of lectures in Paris on *The Invisible and Our Daily Life*. In the flyer he had written:

After having spoken for years on the various fields one discovers when engaged on the path of Christ, I believe the time has come to look at a few practical details, and so in these lectures we will take a closer look at the difficulties met in daily life—difficulties that are the mystic's field of action par excellence, rather than contemplation, meditation, or the labors of "pure spirit."

In April 1913, Sédir took up residence at 31 rue de Seine, commencing what was to be the apogee of his public career. This change coincided with a transformation in his external behavior and appearance. He had always led a bohemian life, to which he brought a natural and rich degree of personal nobility. The physical culture exercises in which he excelled began to transform his figure. He acquired a dog, whom he treated fraternally.

Sédir was always drawn to the lower classes. He held the humble dear, the common people whose lives he had

---

[6] Patron saint of altar servers and first communicants.

shared and with whom he had worked. For this reason he strove to express the highest spiritual truths in their simplest form, so as to be more easily understood by the average person.

It was no doubt for this reason that he decided to speak at the "Popular University" of the Faubourg Saint-Antoine, where on May 11, 1914 he gave a lecture published subsequently as "The True Religion." In the spring of that same year he gave a series of lectures at l'hôtel des Sociétés savantes, about several well-known people. These lectures were later included in the book: *A Few Friends of God*. He also gave a series of twelve conferences on "Soul Culture and Spiritual Development," the closing lecture of which was published in the journal *Psyché* (Jan.–Feb. 1917) under the title: "The Interior Life According to Christ."

Mobilized from 1915–1918 at the War College in the Information Office on Prisoners of War, his apartment became (every night of the week, and Sundays also) a meeting place for soldiers on furlough, their oasis before having to return to the front. Expressed on such occasions were often supreme thoughts on the part of many of our group who were not to return from the front, and would thus take along with them "up there" the peaceful, immutable certitude that their friend and confidant was at pains to impart to them.

Those among us present at that time have no difficulty visualizing Sédir, feeling and experiencing again the blessed atmosphere that the prayers and concentrated life of this servant of God brought down from above. It felt good to be there. His ever-affectionate welcome, offered always with such graciousness, cost him much time, which had to be made up for far into the night.

He spoke little, himself listening untiringly to what we told him. He canalized our thoughts in such as way as to aid us in determining what decision to take—after which, a little later, everything fell into place without our understanding quite how. The concierge would say of him: "He is a very good man," an expression that at first scandalized our veneration for him. And yet, was not this the very best sort of consecration to the earthly values he so wanted us to accept and live by?

Sédir was gifted with a startling faculty of concentration. No matter what the work might be, he did it well and fast. At the office of the War College where he had been mobilized, he became the central focus of activity. Arriving early, he often used to write until the day's work was assigned. One morning he was drafting the Lebanese legend later inserted in his book *The Sermon on the Mount*. At that moment, three ladies employed in the same office, looking for a little fun, began bombarding Sédir with a hail of paper projectiles. I was seated by his side, having been mobilized into the same service. Without discontinuing his writing, he would pick up with his left hand the projectiles that fell within reach and throw them back to his assailants, all the while passing on to me his sheets of writing as he completed them. These pages are among the finest he ever wrote. When he sent them later to the printer, not a single proofreading correction was required.

Here is another memory of the same period. Sédir occasionally said: "I have learned to read diagonally." We often admired the rapidity and sureness with which he would read voluminous scholarly works. Toward the end of the World War we offered him the principal works of Hoene-Wronski—six large volumes in quarto, many pages of which had no text, only large graphs. Moreover, Sédir was still mobilized and working at the War College. Less than three weeks later he delivered to us a highly technical study, ending with a parallel comparison between Wronski, the philosopher of *knowledge*, and his Polish compatriot Towianski,[7] the philosopher of *action*.

⊕

When the war ended, Sédir took up again his apostolate, meetings, and travels.

It was quite natural that those he had directed toward a profound active life gathered around him. They urged him to launch a review as a means of communication as well as a link with sympathizers living further afield in distant provinces or other countries. The first issue of this review, which had been given the name *Bulletin des Amitiés Spirituelles* [Bulletin of the Friends in Spirit] came out in February 1919, summarizing its program with the words: "There surely are to be found lovers of the impossible." Subsequently it was decided to takes steps to set up an association with formal legal standing. Thus it was that on July 16, 1920 there officially appeared in the appropriate legal journal the announcement of the establishment of *Les Amitiés Spirituelles* "as a free and charitable Christian Association." The group of friends who for the past ten years had gradually formed a nucleus around Sédir now had a legal name and charter.

Both men and women had answered Sédir's invitation to work and prayer. Addressing the women as "Marthas and

---

[7] Andrzej Tomasz Towianski (1799–1878), Polish philosopher and messianic religious leader.

Marys," he wrote on their behalf these lines: "I hope to assemble the greatest possible number of servants of the Lord who, whether in their home, at the office, in stores, in palaces, or in garrets, will live to serve God above all, radiating kindness, grace, and serenity." To which he added in their regard:

> Contrary to human associations that grow by increasing the number of members through financial means or through social status, the principle of our association is supernatural: we will not form an assembly; I will not condone any material ties. The spirit will bind you far more than any obligation ever could. Faith increases only in an atmosphere devoid of all earthly certitudes. Unknown to each another, you will then only come to know each other through the radiant shadows of the true faith wherein Christ appears in his integral magnificence. The angel he has chosen to protect this group to which you belong from this day forward will transmit to you his virtues. Your destiny is in your hands. You will triumph in the same measure as you make Jesus your Lord… Like Martha, you will perform your daily tasks, often just as heavy in elegant surroundings as in modest circumstances. Like Mary, you will be consumed from within, sending forth invisible flames, even as you hold in confidence your prayers, your sufferings, and the graces received.

The Friends in Spirit (*Les Amitiés Spirituelles*) have continued to spread the works of Sédir. To its earliest adherents, whom heaven has one by one recalled, new members have been added. And they keep coming, striving to put into practice the teachings of the founder.

## Paul Sédir: by Émile Besson

⊕

On May 30, 1921, Sédir married again, this time to Marie-Jeanne Coffineau, who passed away in October 1938.

During the years following the founding of *Les Amitiés Spirituelles,* Sédir's activity redoubled within the fold of our company: letters, articles, meetings, receptions, conferences in Paris, in many other cities of France, and abroad, notably in Poland, where groups of followers had formed.

Sédir's last public lecture was given November 17, 1925 at the Université Alexandre-Mercereau, boulevard Raspail. That year, after his return from the summer vacation, he stayed with friends living at 33 rue Henri-Heine, in Passy, the sixteenth administrative district of Paris.

On February 3, 1926, after a few days' illness, Sédir was taken from us. A religious service was held at the church of Notre Dame-de-la-Miséricorde. His mortal remains rest in the Saint Vincent cemetery, a few steps away from the rue Girardon, near the tomb of Alice Le Loup.

It is almost a half a century [now a full century] since Sédir left us. But, for his friends, for all those who, close or far away, known or unknown, either gathered together in the bosom of *Les Amitiés Spirituelles* or isolated in their actions and prayer—that is, for all who have found comfort and certitude in his writings—there is before us, as he said himself, "Work for centuries!"

⊕

Just as long ago, before the coming of Christ, prophets announced his coming, so also for the past two thousand years have appeared men and women likewise inspired by heaven—mystic writers whose role has been to bring the gospel within the understanding of their contemporaries,

67

to enlighten them according to the knowledge and insight accessible to their time, and to show them that Christ is always present among us.

Sédir was one of these. He is both a mystic and a modern writer. He stands out from his predecessors in that he speaks and writes as only a man of our time can do, a man fashioned for his mission by exceptional qualities of intellect and heart, by patient labor, by frequenting past and present masters in the field of the sciences of the visible and invisible realms, and lastly (and especially) by having met with an individual in whom, according to his own terminology, he found "a perfect resemblance to Christ."

To seekers of the supernatural whose studies he shared during his youth, to scholars and inventors whose productions and discoveries are ever more startling; to those tempted to glory in their findings—to all these, he has shown that the gospel is the absolute book, that it contains everything, absolutely everything, because it is the word of God.

To those who count the gospel as among the outdated works of the past, or to those who have lost faith and despair of ever finding the light, he proves that the gospel is a living, factual, contemporary book that answers any and all queries and fulfills the daily and fundamental needs of each and every person.

Moreover, Sédir also provides an answer to all who do not feel at ease in churches anymore, all who want to quit the wide highways and take a shortcut, but need to be encouraged and guided. To all who aspire to worship in spirit and truth he says: "You will discover that in the gospel all commandments, all counsels, all maxims, are summed up in one sole order: love our neighbor for the love of God."

## Paul Sédir: by Émile Besson

⊕

For any new readers, the next part of this book will serve as an introduction to the works of Sédir. The chapters contained therein do not figure, except the one on "The Unknown," in his other published books. They include letters, unpublished texts, a lecture, and studies or texts previously printed only in periodicals, back issues of the *Bulletin des Amitiés Spirituelles*, or in works now out of print. These texts recall several well-known aspects of his works. Many letters state his position from within the bosom of the mystic and religious movement. Other letters show to what extent Sédir was a dedicated and trusted guide. Finally, the concluding pages reveal him to have been as enlightened a connoisseur of the masterpieces of art of ancient times as he was also of those of his own time.

# PART II
## Short Works & Articles

# Friends in Spirit

## Les Amitiés Spirituelles

THE Friends in Spirit (*Les Amitiés Spirituelles*) was founded as an association of dedicated persons for the sole purpose of recapturing the spirit of primitive Christianity as way to bring men and women closer to Christ. What binds us together is our recognition of the divinity of Christ and our observance of the gospel. The rest is of no consequence—not race, not religion, not such and such opinions. In fact, Christ declared that "the first and primordial commandment is to love God with all our heart and our neighbor as ourselves."

Here is the declaration of the principles of Friends in Spirit:

> The Association of Friends in Spirit gathers together those (whatever their nationality or religion may be) who recognize Christ as the sole master of the inner life, and the gospel as the true law of consciences and of peoples." It is not a matter of founding a new religion, or yet another sect. The members of this group respect all forms of social custom and religious belief. Nothing exists without its reason and usefulness. Members do not criticize the opinions of others. Their sole desire is to belong to Christ. They are convinced that a real, collective evolution can be obtained only by the spiritual and moral uplifting of each and every

individual, and that the terrible difficulties threatening the Western world today could be overcome if the greatest number of people, on each rung of the social ladder, accomplished more fully their individual duty.

These Friends in Spirit, these *Christian mystics*, profess as their axiom of faith: Jesus Christ, only Son of God, God himself, who came into the world to lead us to eternal life.

Their one and only maxim is to assist others by every means. Their essential sacrament is silent prayer to the only living God, offered in simplicity, confidence, and with joy.

Their ideal is to prepare the human mind, both individually and collectively, to receive the divine light. In consequence, the Friends in Spirit use all their efforts to infuse into their actions the maxims of the gospel. Whether laborers, employees, executives, parents, children, or plain citizens, all endeavor to accomplish their tasks with an honest conscience, to comfort the suffering, and to lessen the misery around them, each within their sphere of action.

Their radiation operates first by prayer and comforting the afflicted, then by word of mouth, and lastly by publishing books. Profoundly convinced that nothing happens without the consent of God, they do not pose as stern reformers. Experience has clearly proven that a helping hand extended to an unfortunate wastrel helps and comforts him far more than does a lecture. They never interfere with other people's conscience, because in their opinion our relations with God are far too solemn and private to require the help of an intermediary.

They ask only that you try on your own account the same experiments they themselves have made. This association belongs to no laic or ecclesiastical organization, nor to any political or secret society. It is averse to political or religious polemics of any kind.

⊕

We believe that the Friends in Spirit have something valuable to offer at this time of universal unrest, which so oppresses the world. They are helping others to turn their attention toward the deliverance that so many of them have lost hope of obtaining.

Sédir has written: "We believe we have found a solution to all problems, a door opening out from all prisons, a remedy to all ills." To which he added: "We offer our discovery to whoever wants to give it a fair try, while respecting the conditions of the experience. It is an old find anyhow! But then, do not old, forgotten remedies often work a better cure than do the most recent ones?"

Moreover, Sédir affirms that, independently of all secret associations and any and all sects, the teaching of Christ has been transmitted down the centuries through an uninterrupted chain of unknown disciples in its pure, perfect, primitive essence. These disciples dispense the solace, relief, and consolations the world has great need of—for they alleviate all grief.

The aim of life is not knowledge. To beings in the Relative it is impossible to grasp, to comprehend, the Absolute. Besides, the intellect is only one of the organs of our total personality. Even at its hypothetical best, it can only offer an image or aspect of life—it is not life itself. Truth is reserved for those who strive to live life, not those who ponder over it, or merely think it. Christ said: "Seek ye first the kingdom of God and the rest will be given unto you."

Our movement is the offspring of brotherhood. We want to be friends. "For us, friendship means worshipping the same ideal, observing the same discipline, and realizing the same activities. And because our ideal is called Christ, our discipline is the gospel, and our activities are good works and prayer. For these reasons, we believe our friendship to be the purest, the loftiest, the staunchest."

Among our membership there is no centralization of authority giving instructions. Each person is free to act as he pleases and is solely answerable to God. Each must feel responsible for the entire movement.

We attack no one, we criticize no one, for we are convinced that all that lives has the right to live, and that what is evil will disappear of itself when the time is ripe. Naturally, we express our opinions whenever we are asked, and proclaim what we believe to be true, but we never impose our opinions upon others.

The gospel always stresses moral principles, ethics, and piety. Never does it refer to scientific or philosophical research. Sédir has explained this viewpoint in his brochure "The Gospel and the Problem of Knowledge," where he points out how the disciple of Christ has the right to make use of his mind alongside a concurrent duty to confine this activity within definite limits. The trap into which intellectuals risk falling is insatiability, which is "as deleterious to them as it is to businessmen who work themselves to death in order to acquire a fortune."

Spiritual poverty alone makes us susceptible of receiving instruction from above. When a man is in that state, he perceives unknown lights. Instead of forms and law, the very archetypes reveal to him their essence. Hence, he sees the spirit of things, the spirit of beings, their central relationships, and their permanent simplicity.

Candidates for "initiation," on the other hand, fancying themselves belonging to an elite, believe they can stride forth into realms to which ordinary searchers have no access. They imagine that through their own powers they might escape the finite, pass beyond the conditioned.

The Friends in Spirit, however, have one objective only: to reiterate the teachings of the gospel, of the bible. They do not seek to dominate nature. Neither do they desire to do so. The heart is the true center of man; his mentality and sensitivity are but instruments.

What distinguishes divine truth from human truths is that the latter are merely points of view and approximations. In any case, they are theoretical affirmations without any immediate connection with life. Divine truth, on the other hand, not being a doctrine, but a life, is a life that develops and realizes itself in the same degree to which it is lived.

We believe that the highest philosophical speculations are not worth the glass of water given to a fevered patient. In fact, by acting that way we are only following the example of Christ. He could have remained in his kingdom and launched from there some currents of sympathy and comfort upon our dolorous and straying humanity. He could have sent angels, prophets, and sages to relieve our distress. But he preferred to come here-below himself. Of all solutions that the formidable problem of redemption entailed, he chose the one where he had to give the most of himself. He has been the good shepherd who looks for the straying ewe until he finds her. And at the end of a life of love and sacrifice, he condensed his teaching and all of his examples into the words: "As I have loved you, love ye one another."

Such is our faith, such is our motto. And this imitation of Jesus Christ is not the privilege of either an elite or a social caste; it is accessible to any creature of good will.

The kingdom of God is not composed of an aristocracy of intellectuals; it is for all. Christ said that one day there will be only one flock, under the leadership of the sole Shepherd. And he showed us the way: "They will know you as my disciples if you love one another."

Also, the master of Sédir said: "You will not be asked what you believed in, but what you have done."

⊕

It is written: "You will know the tree by its fruits." And Christ declared: "If you dwell in me, and if my words dwell in you, what you ask for will be given you."

It behooves us not to reveal things that must remain secret. But those who have lived close to Sédir have witnessed healings, deliverances, and illuminations that "circumstances" could not explain.

We are not invited to explain God, but to make an effort towards God. Sédir used to tell his friends: "We spend our life giving to God what He does not ask for, and we do not give Him that for which He asks."

God wants from us a great deal more than our piety, godly customs, orthodox doctrines, or beautiful words! He wants our whole heart, our every thought: He wants our life in its entirety.

Beethoven used to say: "Each man loves in his own way." To which Sédir added: "But each must love as much as he can."

He who does not love is not a disciple of Christ, even were he to speak his name. He who does not forgive trespasses is not condemned by God; rather, he condemns himself, precisely because he asks God to forgive him as he forgives others. The man who does not love, the man who does not surpass himself to reach out and understand human suffering and try to bring it solace, that man, whether he be scholar, artist, moralist, or social leader, is nothing before God; and before man he merely exemplifies and exudes hard-heartedness.

There are indeed people who cannot believe in Christ when they see the life led by some who claim to be disciples of Christ.

From time immemorial, the mystical life has been compared to a summit that must be ascended. Those who have attempted to scale it have discovered such horizons and received such intimate impressions and certitude that the desire to share the joys granted them was ignited. But how could mere accounts or narratives succeed in making felt any of the realities experienced or blessings received? How could they enable the atmosphere of the mountain, or the panorama revealed from its summit, to seep into our lungs or fill our eyes?

What Sédir has written on mystical life is but the account of a traveler who went on to conquer the peak, the goal of humanity's millennial efforts. If for over thirty years he gave lectures and wrote books, it was with the hope that his words would awaken in some mind, in some heart, the desire to undertake the mystical ascent. If he describes landscapes, forewarns of precipices, exults in the joy of the ascent, it is because he hopes that what has given him the certitude of intelligence and peace of heart may give to others that same certitude and peace. Those who remain at the foot of the mountain—the lukewarm, the timid, the dilettantes—do not know the aesthetic pleasure of aspiring towards the ultimate. They do not feel a desire for a loftier life. They do not know the infinitely noble labors of the ascension. To know spiritual realities merely through the intellect is to have a bogus, warped knowledge. It is as if merely studying the geographical map of a mountain could reveal to you the horizons to be admired from its summit.

Assuredly, to make the ascent one must first find the road to the mountain on the map. But then, with a knapsack on one's back, one must commence the climb.

# The Friends of God

## *in Modern Society**

HEN WE LOOK around us, we see nothing but feverish haste, lust for power, greed, avarice, lewdness, cunning, vanity, brutality. Values are measured in money; jealousy and rancor reign. We say this over and over to ourselves monotonously. It cheapens our dignity. Why not get away for a few minutes from these stifling surroundings? Since reality oppresses us, let us go for a spell to the great spaces in the realm of dream, there where pure and simple forms waft by, the landscape is harmonious, and zephyrs sigh among the branches.

And since we are free to roam in this marvelous world of imagination, why not choose the most beautiful and most sublime of dreams, the one in which the fervor of artists, the thoughts of philosophers, and the desires of simple men who simply seek happiness join together—in short, the dream humankind has been pursuing from the very beginning, the dream of the divine? But consider: because this dream seems to us by far the most unattainable, most impossible of dreams, and because extremes meet, might not this dream in fact be the closest, the most attainable, of dreams; indeed, the one easiest to experience?

* Lecture given at Rouen, Oct. 12, 1919

⊕

Among the multitude of men and women are some who
live on spiritual peaks. Such innocent beings confined to a
limited world, such voluntary victims in an aggressive
world, who find their peace in what provokes the anger of
others, who seek silence as others seek renown, who lie in
wait for trials or pain as others thirst for pleasure—such
beings as these must remain enigmas to any who do not
join their school.

Everyone loves someone or something. Everyone spends
great effort to attain power, or whatever they want. Some,
the true elite, work without personal or monetary gain in
view. Among these are the "Unknowns" I want to acquaint
you with. Their total self-abnegation stems from their penetrating insight. Where the philanthropist sees nothing but
a sequence of vices, poor heredity, ignorance, or bad education; where the sociologist deplores the consequences of
inopportune laws; where the thinker becomes sad and discouraged—these "Unknowns" of whom I am speaking see
nothing more than a weakness of the flesh or an embittered
spirit. They are, so to say, obstinate in their hopefulness
because they are certain they can offer solace or healing,
because they are certain that they can see—behind laziness,
perversions, and turpitudes—the inextinguishable glow of
the lamp of eternity, for which even the least among men
serves as a perpetual tabernacle.

These lovers of the absolute are not dilettantes and amateurs of marvels, or seekers after curiosities. On the contrary, they prefer lofty thoughts to stupendous marvels. For
them, a bowl of soup offered to the poor glorifies God far
more than does the lengthy litany of a Pharisee. They are
not preoccupied with their personal salvation. Neither do

they seek rest—they seek work. Foremost, in all things and in every place, they perceive God, whose flashing splendor transfigures all ugliness and all vices, fathoms every abyss, drains all swamps.

Are such "Unknowns" overly proud in believing themselves collaborators of the Supreme Being? Of course not! For this very collaboration belongs solely to the humble, the "poor in spirit," who are well aware of the scope of human ignorance. Must they, then, be feeble-minded? Of course not! For all humankind has been fed by this same dream, refreshed by these same hopes.

⊕

Each day we see crowds surging into movie theaters rather than storming the exhibition of works of art or listening to the performance of a musical masterpiece. In most fields, mediocrity carries off the prize. It is not surprising, then, to find so few true servants of heaven in the religious field. They are rare indeed. Some seek God in books. Others look for Him in soul spheres or in occult experiences. Both will find the answer as soon as they recognize that peace is solely the gift of self; that true, living understanding is obtained once we have taken the measure of our ignorance; that mysteries finally reveal their secrets the instant we have fulfilled our destiny. Such are the points of departure of the Friend of God toward his interior life.

Businessmen live to launch enterprises, to win for themselves a place in the sun. Scientists live to accumulate incontrovertible facts, as many as they can. Philosophers assemble these facts according to their common denominators, classify them, bring out their analogies, extend them to other hypotheses derived from the results of numerous experiments. Artists seek to bring to light from living forms their most intense signification. Contemplative mystics treat the visible world as a stepping-stone to the invisible realm, where they linger as often as they can. Friends of God, however, see only expedients in all these goals. Through all such experiential phenomena, system-building, and inner illuminations, they slash and cut right through to the Absolute. And because the Absolute is found at the center of all the worlds (and of all parts of all the worlds), the remarkable, foolhardy Friends of God maintain their equilibrium; and when upon the earth, are just as ready for ecstasies as for positive works.

The most accomplished practical achievers have their secret weaknesses. The loftiest thinkers affirm that they know nothing. The most rigid ascetics can just be stubborn men. Devils can have a faith. It can be that magicians conjure through dark forces. Seers may see in error. The most active apostles may be nothing but ambitious men. In short, the sole true mark of the veritable mystic, the Friend of God, is love.

But to perceive beauty, its reflection must have been inwardly received. Similarly, to discern divine love in the heart of one of our brothers, one must remain unknown. That is why the Friends of God remain unknown. Only their peers know them. Perhaps we see them in action, but since we are unable to perceive their motives, we attribute false ones to them, so that they are misjudged by the world. In any case, they never defend themselves. They are voluntary dupes, benevolent men whom others exploit. They claim that good done in secret is more efficacious, and propagates best. Now, this opinion, opposite to that of philanthropists, is the opinion of Christ. The "advantage" it offers is that of attracting calumnies and slander. But these peculiar men, these unknown Friends of God, do not mind being targets of their neighbors' taunts. They, who take all things seriously, smile when they are attacked. I have known one who lived in a large city, about whom people circulated rumors of swindles and fraud. "Bah," he used to tell me, "people have to talk about something; they will keep quiet when they run out of anything else to say. And besides—between us—they will never tell as much evil about me as I think about myself."

⊕

This might seem to be an affectation of humility; but no, this man was sincere. Let me try to help you understand his state of mind. You have certainly met people who possess an avid mind and a good memory. Such people read whatever comes their way. They stock up on theories, but do not themselves know how to think, to weigh ideas, to form an opinion. If it should happen that some metaphysical problem is outlined to such people, they will "solve" it then and there. Their answer may not hold true, but this makes no difference—they will cling to it like grim death.

As an example let us take a man universally renowned for his penetrating intelligence: the philosopher Henri Bergson.[1] Bergson has read everything. He is up-to-date with discoveries in chemistry, biology, sociology, anthropology, and every other "-logy" that may exist. In one of his books he relates the following anecdote with the candor of a thoughtful man who expresses himself straightforwardly. It

---

[1] Henri Bergson, French philosopher 1854–1941, Académie Francaise; Nobel Prize, 1927.

happened in a salon. One of the greatest medical experts of the day was expounding a theory on the mechanism of consciousness. When the expert had finished his presentation, a young woman approached Bergson and said: "I listened very carefully to Prof. X. It seems to me he makes an error, but I cannot figure out where." Bergson, although an undisputed master of philosophy, might well have just ignored that young woman's problem, but he took note of it instead, pondered upon it, and a few days later discovered for himself the false reasoning of that professor of psychology.

So it is that the more accomplished a man is in any field, the more modest he is, the better he measures the extent of all he has still to master, the more he pays attention to small things. The man of God does not conduct himself otherwise. The nearer he draws to his ideal, the better he measures the distance separating him from it; the better he appreciates the obstacles, the better he realizes both the importance of small efforts and the gravity of small omissions. That is why saints are severe with themselves, why they are so desolate over shortcomings that we would barely notice.

⊕

It is not the public life of their master that the Friends in Spirit seek to emulate, it is his private life. The disciple of Christ does not wear oriental garb, is not a soap-box orator, does not play at being a mage. The true mystic is first of all a sensible man. Common sense is perhaps more indispensable in spiritual life than it is in everyday life.

The epithet "mystic" is often misunderstood. Too bad! It should never be taken to mean psychic disequilibrium. To the contrary, the mystic strives to become healthy before attempting to become a saint. Those whose goal is to penetrate the invisible and perform marvels are no mystics, but poor, over-curious, vain men. The word "mystic" means secret, inexpressible, incommunicable—hence, whatever is beyond analytic understanding, is felt only by the soul, heart, or feeling center.

And so, everything has its mysticism. War has its mysticism: honor, glory, and patrimony. The Republicans of 1789 and 1848 were such mystics. Michelangelo's *Slaves* are mystical; Bouguereau's *Virgins* are not. Corneille is a mystic in every way; Racine in *Athalie* is not.

There are souls for whom even the totality of all that is capable of being communicated would still fall short of filling the void. Such souls thirst for the Absolute. Beyond the most exalted words, it is Speech incarnate, the Word, that they want to hear. Beyond masterpieces of art, it is Beauty itself that they want to contemplate. Through all forms, within all desires, at the core of all ideals, it is the Absolute that they want to reach. It is God they are looking at; it is for His benevolence they want to pave the way.

These souls I speak of emulate the Lord. To serve him, nothing seems too difficult. For them, struggles, failures, are nothing. What touches them most is the effusion pouring from their sacrificed heart, liquefied upon the flames of love. Jesus, with his own hands, ignited this inextinguishable fire within them. That is why, over and over again, they surrender themselves to him with renewed prayers. They try to do more and more to serve him, never ceasing.

These secret disciples know that their Master did not weigh the cost (debauchery, rebuffs, moral and physical tortures) of making contact with men; and so they strive to establish the same contact in order to reach their still deaf brothers. They are fraternal toward the weak, indulgent to the vicious, compassionate to the sorrowful. They practice privations and accept renunciations, taking it upon themselves to experience ingratitude in order all the better to sympathize with the unfortunate, to speak to them heart to heart. And they spare no effort to silence a complaint or to soothe a grudge. Such are their private lives, their hidden lives, the deep-rooted labor to which they submit.

⊕

The wonderful word "compassion" (prostituted, as most other great words are) opens the widest perspectives to their hearts. To be compassionate means "to suffer with." It means taking up another's load. It means undertaking to steer the pitiable heart we meet with grave, beatifically tender sympathy. It means giving of oneself.

Some people organize meetings and issue manifestos. The Friends of God offer love and solace without fanfare. They are the evokers of the all-goodness, and for these "lay eucharists" offer themselves as both priests and victims. The poles between which they oscillate are prayer and acts of charity, thus uniting (as Jesus desires) the most vigorous action with man's most vital living dream.

"I have given you the example," said Jesus, "that you do as I did for you . . . you are my friends if you do what I command. This is my commandment, that you love one another as I have loved you; there is no greater love than to give one's life for a friend." Jesus does not profess: he commands. He propounds no theories, abstractions, or symbols: he wants deeds. Thus, his disciples, clear-headed yet with blazing hearts, seek the most intense activity. Now, to act contrary to our imaginations demands more energy than giving in to them; to act with an ideal as our goal demands more courage than to lean toward an advantageous personal result; to act in obedience to God (obedience meaning love) is purer than to act for the love of some person. This is what the activity of disciples consists of, as it finds full expression in works of love. Their method is love, their radiation is love, their power is love.

Love is a living chain binding God to man, drawing man up to God, gathering all living creatures together into one flock. Love is a living flame. Its ardor and brilliancy are magnified in proportion to the obstacles they encounter. The heart upon which one of the sparks of this flame falls remains ablaze forever. Fused into incandescence, this heart irrigates its surroundings just as water from an inexhaustible spring does the fields through which it flows.

Pure love does not tarry in mystical consolations or ecstasies. It soars. It hovers, its unmoving, gliding wings outspread like those of the great eagles of craggy solitudes on the watch for some miserable, sad being, ready to pounce upon him and carry him forth with effortless vigor toward the serene, resplendent empyreans of the eternal sun. Because love gives itself wholly each time, the life of love is an uninterrupted sequence of deaths. It is also a sequence of rebirths, because love is the essence of life.

Knowing that each moment discloses the will of the Father, love feeds upon grief and afflictions—since they are the mystical body of the Word. "My food," says Jesus, "is to do the will of the One who sent me." The disciples know that Jesus still works and suffers, that a compassionate gesture made in some corner of the globe is transfigured and ascends to cool the feverish mouth of the perpetual martyr, that a wound dressed on earth stanches the blood of the crucified (the crucified, still relentlessly tortured by the millions of ignominies committed by men)—the blood of this agonizing victim, who cannot die and does not want to die.

He said "What you do to the poor in my name, is done unto me." The disciples know that this is rigorously true, that it is the exact truth. The unfortunate one who suffers, perhaps in revolt, is without doubt not Christ; but the moment a Friend of God extends a hand of solace, by its powerful virtue of compassion something within this hapless, heavy-laden wretch meets a ray of the irradiating Word, and begins its ascent toward heaven. Everything comes from Christ, everything returns to Christ. Through him, the least charitable act performed by those who love him becomes a masterpiece. Through him, joys become sorrows, and sorrows joys.

We are unaware of this kind of love. We believe we love our wives, husbands, children, and country. But it is ourselves we love in them. And yet this selfish, insecure love does occasionally lift us up to heroism. What would we not attain, then, were we to love them for themselves—forgetting ourselves? If we loved them in God? The Master of love tells us how to go about attaining this purity—by doing good, primarily to those for whom we feel antipathy.

In fact, we can truly grow only when we surpass ourselves, when we emerge from our limitations. Our true homeland is the supernatural state we will re-enter only after having gotten rid of our natural inclinations, our selfishness—to be accomplished by systematic efforts, by devoting ourselves to accepting the repugnant chores no one wants to be burdened with, by helping those the world shuns, by taking an interest in and comforting the incurables and incorrigibles.

Almsgiving is more fruitful when given from our necessi-

ιore potent than hair-shirts or scourges, better
or lengthy prayers, are physical fatigues resulting
from our charitable deeds—which are far more efficacious
in bringing solace down from heaven. Yes, quietly praying
at home for a sick person is less painful than going up to his
garret, sweeping it clean, preparing meals, and changing
bandages, but such care radiates a light that changes a state
of soul and mind better than merely prayerful exhortations.

⊕

The Word gives himself to whoever likewise gives himself.
The Friends of God are the true "poor in spirit," the true
poor according to the spirit. A millionaire may be poor
before the Lord, and a beggar a millionaire. This is true in
many ways, under many conditions, according to several
points of view. But let us look just now at one: the only one
that lies within our reach.

Our Friends of God take no credit for their inborn gifts,
knowing full well that these gifts do not belong to them,
that they neither purchased nor acquired them, that the
very energy thanks to which they cultivated these gifts was
itself a gift also—or at least a recompense far surpassing
what they merited. Our Friends, being convinced of these
things, possess these gifts as if they did not possess them,
such as might some extraordinary stockholder who worries
neither over fluctuations of the stock market nor thieves.
Our Friends, inordinately rich intellectually, filled with
energy and ingenuity, really are poor—because the senti-
ment of ownership has no place in their hearts. This is why
supernatural plenitudes pour in to fill them. Because they
stand naked before glory, the inconceivable virtues of the
spirit clothe them magnificently. Accustomed, as they are,

to the startling "tenebrae" of faith,[2] they perceive the true forms of beings. They receive knowledge, power, and beatitude, without deviation, reflection, or intermediaries.

When the spirit takes hold of a man and lifts him up to the sun of thought, or to the sun of beauty, what that man will later relate to other men is known as genius. When the spirit gathers up a man agonizing in his desire for God, and when he bathes him, restores him, and quenches his thirst at the eternal spring, this man, from then on, in his language and gaze, his gestures and silences, his smiles and tears, his labors and sleep (in short, the whole man)—that man, in his entire being, is in the state of sanctity.

Such are the Friends of God. They live in the spirit. Through the spirit they foresee the future, even as they also clearly see the past. It is through the spirit that they protect, heal, and enlighten. How is it done? Our catechism teaches that there are seven gifts of the Holy Spirit, which theologians explain at great length. But if they could be explained, they would not be gifts of the spirit anymore. They would be forces of nature, more or less subtle, more or less understood. As a matter of fact, if one does not possess those gifts, one cannot talk about them; and if one does possess them, one dare not talk about them—for no none would understand.

An electrician switches on a current. He knows what it is; he analyzes it for you. He is more or less its master. A man of letters explains how and why beautiful verses move you. A magnetist brings about certain phenomena in a subject, regarding which he knows—or rather states—some plausible theories. But no one can comprehend the substance of

---

[2] An experience known among mystics as the night of the soul.

supernatural gifts. Only their effects may be perceived, like the wind of the spirit that blows where it wills. The Spirit penetrates his chosen ones, his blessed victims, unexpectedly, deep down, through their consciousness, above and below, everywhere at once, or through some imperceptible gap: you never know. Then he radiates outwards so subtly and suddenly that those whose foreheads bear one or the other of the Spirit's seven crowns are not even aware of it.

Do not the greatest before God believe themselves to be unworthy? Do we not notice the vanity of the half-baked scientist compared to the modesty of the true scholar?

⊕

But, I do not want to penetrate any deeper into the inner life of the Friends of God. "My secret belongs to me," answered St Theresa to a prying Dominican. These Friends keep the secret of their agreements with God; whoever willingly tells about himself, also admits what he knows about others; and besides, while the secrets of science or politics need to be guarded, the secrets of the inner life guard themselves. Discretion among true disciples of the gospel emanates throughout their entire personality in their conduct. These ardent men may seem indifferent—so strong is their concern not to impose themselves or to remove anyone from his chosen path. They do not take part in political strife, because they do not believe in politics. They do not take part in social activism because in their eyes all possess a legitimate claim.

They have no personal axe to grind in these questions. Since they work for God, they are persuaded that God will furnish them what is necessary. They neither seek fortune nor fame. They believe there is no injustice—that visible injustice is but an invisible justice the reason for which escapes them. But, wiser than I in this instance, they do not say so! In short, they believe that if each citizen would reduce his ambitions and covetousness to his legitimate share, live a respectable dignified life both at home and in business, the question of social peace would be resolved better than by vociferous propaganda.

We, on the contrary, being practical people, in times of shortages try to seduce the grocer, start hoarding sugar without scruples—too bad about the others who will shop later! The Friend of God would have qualms about depriving an old man of sugar. That thought stops him. He is more logical than his fellow citizens. Censuring violence and ruse in others, he strongly forbids himself their use. Is he a simpleton? Or might he be a just man?

Logically put, this just man fulfills justice by obeying. He obeys God, whose command he sees everywhere. He knows that nothing occurs without God's permission and that God permits only what is useful for us. Hence he obeys regulations, laws, and—what is still more difficult—all the agents of these diverse authorities. You would probably smile, seeing him endure the caprices of some functionary. Just remember the difficulties you may have had with porters at a station, or train conductors. Do you recall the effort you had to make when asked to pay some piddling overcharge and the effort you should have deployed so as not to show your annoyance? The Friend of God pays and smiles. He thinks that whoever is not capable of overcoming little things will never achieve great ones. Napoleon I was of the same mind; you will find that explained in his *Memorial from St Helena*. It is merely another point upon which mystics and realists agree.

In the eyes of one who belongs to God, the universe unfolds as a gigantic scroll on which angels have inscribed providential decrees, from the greatest to the least. Faith minutely outlines the course of his conduct in advance. Moreover, he is the disciple of a Master who, without being obliged to, obeyed infinitely. Jesus suffered all the natural sequences of life: the limitations of childhood, hunger, sleep, customs, functionaries, Pharisees, and Romans. Jesus *is* essentially a perpetual act of obedience.

Therefore, the Friends of God will not be the ones to attack or to scorn any religious expressions. They believe that rites lose their operative value if they are not animated by love and nourished with good works. Far from ravishing souls from the gates of glory, the automatic performance of sacraments is a triple sin of laziness, of a lie, and of profanation. Our mystics are well aware that multitudes have committed these errors, but they prefer to ignore them. They act as if they did not know. They neither reprimand nor criticize. They encourage. They are living examples of something better. They want to see nothing but good. They probe into the heart of a wretch for the remnants of beauty still within him, so as to help them rise to the surface. Their task is not to make others work but to work for others, to shoulder the load of the weak, to rekindle the lukewarm, to restore harmony. In imitation of the patient gardener who does not break off the half-cropped branch, they abstain from criticisms and controversies.

Jesus has no need of professors or apologists. He needs apostles, laborers in his vineyard, men who through their action give testimony to the veracity of his words—that his word is truth. Finally, conforming to their Master, true disciples conform to the customs of their time. They do not affect singularity or scandalize, but approach life with inalterable optimism.

⊕

Each man is indebted to others: to his village, province, and country; to his race and religion; to the visible and invisible worlds; to his ancestors and friends; to God. The challenge he faces is to acquit himself with goodwill. Therefore, is it not important that the Master's workers set an example with alacrity and optimism in order to obtain the same reflexes of goodwill from others? They will conceal their weariness from others so as to better lead the fold toward hope, toward successively tangible hopes. The satisfaction of the crowd is thus made out of the sweat and travail of a few voluntary innocent victims. Unlike Solomon, they think that *every* day brings something new under the sun; and that *nothing*, or almost nothing, has yet been said. They know that all error fights for truth; and that at the door of the Mystic Vine, those who come forward are told: "You who enter here, leave all despair behind you."

To give you more of a sense for the grandeur of these extraordinary beings, I am obliged to depict their tribulations. And yet, whether they are poor or ill-clothed, whether their future is uncertain and their nights are spent worrying about the unfortunates they minister to—still a mysterious joy dwells in the depths of their hearts. It is generally believed that Christ forbids us to be merry, because he desires us to renounce the self. That is wrong. Does he not affirm that joy in sacrifice is perfect joy? And if our terrestrial or human delights always leave behind a bitter taste, is it not because their primal pretexts are based upon what is perishable? We definitely feel that eternal values alone give us serenity. In spite of our strayings and divagations, there persists within us a gnawing memory of a frontierless country that, beyond the stars, spreads out its marvelous landscapes under ever-shining suns. There, resplendent forms never clothe perverted minds; there, perfumes waft out from pure substances; there, the harmony of its music truly expresses the harmony of souls.

Yes, this dream is real. This nostalgia is legitimate and our hopes steadfast. We do not hope; we do not have sufficient fervor; we do not desire that dream with sufficient constancy. Meanwhile, the Friends of God, whose renunciations have increased their energy tenfold, know how to will and possess that dream. For them it becomes a reality, since they incarnate it in their lives. We see some of these wandering knights of the ideal, we notice the apparent misery of their existence, the mud that spatters over them. Subjected to the vulgarities that jostle them, they seem very much like us. But we do not see their true existence, their interior life. No one guesses that their souls inhabit the clear skies of spiritual realms amid the smiling merriment of angels and saints.

They know their Master loves them. Happy to be captives of love, nothing can wound them mortally; they are settled in love as into an impregnable fortress. Well aware that crowds dislike precursors, they expect anything to happen. They know what God desires, and they do it. Their soul savors the taste of the mystical wine that is love. Through the joys love brings them, they appreciate their precious poverty. They feel strong due to the strength of the Master to whom they gave themselves. They feel invincible, for they know the victory of love to be a certainty. How could they be anything but happy and blessed?

⊕

Their kindness devoid of self-interest, their hearty welcome, their optimism, their immutable joy, give these disciples of Christ an "open sesame" power to enter into people's hearts. But they do not make use of it; they enter only when the doors are open. To enter into a heart is such a grave task! Those who believe themselves (though unworthily) to be the instruments of God assume a very heavy task and function. They condemn themselves to a dual task. First, to do the work of the common man, which in itself is already complicated and stressful (we mean the daily grind of all fathers and mothers, laborers, employees, employers—in short, of all citizens). How vast and tiresome this work is, since it must be resumed each day! Secondly, to fulfill the work of the Christian, which means work beyond the first, above the first, and in the interstices of the first. It is an overwhelming task. Although the same in its outer form as the work of any good man, it is more subtle, has another essence, another quality. The same work, but fulfilled by a different kind of soul, whose hands are filled with blessings, whose limpid eyes are imbued with light.

Though on the surface the disciple seems merely a good man, inwardly and unbeknownst to himself he is on a platform. The spirits of other men are riveted upon him. He is a leader. He is more than others—that much stronger and wiser in the measure that he believes himself less than others. Lastly, he is the elder brother. Because he belongs to Christ, a subtle radiation makes him stand out. Without trying to, he radiates. His actions and thoughts carry further than those of others, and in secret ways. Therefore, he is ruthless towards himself. The slightest deviation or digression that would seem insignificant to us is for him a grave error, one that he rigorously checks. To radiate peace, must he not secure it first in himself?

This is the secret of the disciples' strength—they are masters of themselves, and they possess this mastery because of humility and not through pride. They consider themselves nullities, but nullities that plenitude fills to overflowing. Any inner cause of discord is annihilated in them, and no outer cause can ever trouble them. They give whatever is asked of them. Regardless of who makes the request—to them they bestow. Inspiration, decision, and gesture are all one to them. Thought, feeling, and action are all one. Because they think in the name of Christ, and because they labor in the name of Christ, their being is one. Their personality is an homogeneous block, similar to those scintillating, translucid stones from which St John claims the city of God is built. They do not *seem* to be; they *are* at first sight. Their humility and self-effacement should render their character seemingly insipid; yet, no one is more impassive than they—devoid of contraction and rigidity. I have known some during the war, some after peace was signed. You are aware that there exist many kinds of courage, that one can be a hero in the trenches and a coward when facing a bill due; a man may be an intellectual giant but a coward physically; lastly, how rare it is to find in one man an equal measure of physical courage, moral courage, and intellectual courage! The Friends I have known possessed, if I may express myself thus, integral courage. Everything to them seemed to be God-sent. Beneath the vilest ignominies, their eyes could only detect the divine ray by means of which they exist. The impossible did not exist before their serenity, and a mere smile of theirs brought strength to the fearful, and qualms regarding mysteries to the sceptics.

Thus, possessing certitude, sincerity, and solidity, these servants of God bring about the fulfillment of their strength through patience. They neither act in haste nor are they indolent; they know each minute to be precious. They also know their Master to be master of time. Nothing disheartens them, nothing seems negligible. They do not impose their views; they scrupulously respect others' consciences. They are content to drop a word here and there, and to set a good example most of the time. If their interlocutor, benevolent yesterday, shows signs of becoming refractory today, they keep silent—but implore truth to descend upon him.

These men of action are also men of prayer. As God has given them the right of importuning Him, they make use of it—one could even say that they abuse that right, were it possible to abuse God! When they have judged that God should heal a certain patient, or come to the help of a destitute man, they do not let go until that has been granted. It is for this reason that they often earn the reputation of being magicians, healers, and seers. But they reject these titles. They do not want it said that they perform miracles. For them, miracles are not extraordinary. Rather, they are simple, because miracles occur daily. But theirs is a dedication or self-sacrifice one does not find daily; and that kind of dedication is of far greater interest to them.

Because they would like to lead men toward happiness— the liberation they know to be desirable and real—they are hunters of souls, trappers whose snares are undetectable, fools whose wisdom will be made manifest on the great Judgment Day. They are the faithful dogs of the great Shepherd, who relentlessly harass the straying flock, the unmanageable he-goats, and the docile ewes. Their fate is to be cudgeled or thrashed by cruel farmers, pantingly running obstacle-races, being sore and weary. They toil throughout the world unknown, disparaged, unrecognized, slighted, exhausted, starved—yet nothing fazes them. What matters to them is to please the Master, so that on the last night, they will safely bring back to him the flock entrusted to their care.

⊕

This may seem fantastic, perhaps! You might even believe that I kept my promise to lead you for a while to the land of Utopia. But no, that I have not done; I have remained in the world of reality. These extraordinary beings I have just mentioned live as we do, and we may bump up against one on the street. It is not in inaccessible temples, in antediluvian crypts, in desert caves that you will encounter them, but where life abounds, the masses toil, the factory smoke-stacks spew out pollutants masking the sky—wherever man's prosaic struggles remain. Must it not be that way in order that, in coming to its orbit's term, the world does not roll into the primeval chaos? Must there not be compensation to balance all our thriving selfishness? Is not an impetus toward heaven better than our catapulting into hells? Is it not necessary—before the great hearths around which the hallucinations of matter sing, before the cold lamps of knowledge—to have a few living sparks of eternal light?

We need martyrs of good will to balance the excesses of those who do no more than enjoy themselves. We need madmen of God, since there are so many madmen of the ego; we need sacrifices, since there are murderers; we need beings of gentleness and tenderness in the face of the violent; we need sleepless prayers, since so many vigils are for cunning and debauchery; we need invincible wills straining toward the Ideal, which is the only Real, since so many passions rush towards an illusion they take for the real.

"Such men do not exist," you will probably say. "Abnegation so total, so general, so constant, so genial; such a force remaining unsung, such goodness without human self-interest—such cannot exist, it has never been seen." Pardon me, it has been seen, it does exist! If it did not exist, you would not have permitted me to speak of it to you. At my very first words you would have left, your common sense would have revolted. But you did listen. Hence, in spite of yourself perhaps, something deeply ingrained knew it to be true. Something experienced a long time ago brought back the remembrance of having seen and experienced such love, and an analogous force, in the beginning of time. However, if such a state of soul exists somewhere within us, or outside us, it means we can realize it. It means we can make it descend, first into our conscience, then into our acts. If I were permitted to lift the veil of the secrets of history, how many admirable lives would reveal their hidden grandeur. But God does not want the virtues of His Friends to be revealed to the world, except in the light of the last day.

That is why I have merely given you generalities; but it was my duty to do so. The simple evocation of these immemorial memories, the palest reflection of these lights, even its clumsiest exploitation—may awaken one heart languishing in lethargy. Such is my hope; and perhaps naively, but very sincerely, I believe this hope will not be disappointed.

# An Unknown

N O MATTER HOW sublime were the Friends of
God we have just contemplated, they might not
satisfy certain devotees of the Absolute. Perhaps
one of them adopts a sharp tone or rigid attitude that disappoints some friends as being characteristics
of human frailty. Perhaps another's contemplation, or the
sublime heights he attains, might blind him to the glory of
adjoining summits. Perhaps yet another retreats too far,
leaving behind the pitiful, trampling crowds in which we
live. Or else perhaps the inebriating atmosphere of certain
altitudes has lifted another beyond himself—so much so,
that when he redescends his exaltation disconcerts us.

Would the bread of angels be too rich a food, or the
water of eternal springs too potent a beverage? No. Contrary to general opinion, I am certain it is possible to maintain harmonious poise within ourselves even as we follow
the most rigorous asceticism. I would like to present to you
the living proof of this paradox. And I take the liberty of
affirming that I have for a long time had the privilege of
knowing a man who, without any apparent effort, realized
the perfection of the gospel. It is an arduous task indeed to
try to depict such a rare and complex personality, and I will
certainly not come up to my task. But I trust the same
desire for spiritual beauty that compels me to total frank-
ness, and that animates us one and all, will also fill the gaps
and the clumsiness of my account.

Avoiding curiosity seekers, refusing polemics, mute in face of calumnies, imposing silence on his disciples' enthusiasm—this admirable man whose stirring radiance I would like to make perceptible to you always took extreme precautions to remain anonymous. I believe it would ill serve his purpose to reveal his identity. Biographical details are unnecessary when they concern an individual whose formation was singularly exempt from racial as well as environmental influences. I never would have undertaken the present study had I not felt obliged to give a truthful testimony of the constancy of divine promises in an epoch where all chimeras don such seductive colors. Perhaps a few troubled souls will find courage again if one of their comrades affirms that the promises of Christ are real, because he has seen and assayed their experiential proofs. Christ our Lord once said that he would give his Friends the power to accomplish greater miracles than his. I have seen it fulfilled. Christ also told his Friends that he would remain among them till the end of time. I have seen that hidden presence. The life of my Unknown is but a series of such proofs. Through what little I dare tell you, you will recognize in him, I hope, one of the mysterious "brothers" of the Lord, one of the greatest, the greatest perhaps, of the heralds of the Absolute.

⊕

One had to observe the man closely to discover the diverse privileges belonging to celebrated mystics—his personality harmonizing them so thoroughly, his manner being so simple, as if forgetful of such magnificent prerogatives. His kindly patriarchal greeting and the language he used, even at moments that to common judgment seemed solemn, showed how human grandeur and earthly tragedies are small in comparison to the works of God, whose immense and ever-renovated splendor absorbed his gaze. If we can imagine a being capable of retaining his equilibrium on all points wherein the infinite enters in the finite, it will help elucidate for us all the contradictions that our personage willingly accumulated. Familiar with most, inaccessible to a few; daring and prudent, meticulous or hasty; speaking as a poet at times or as a businessman at others; knowing secrets stretching to eternity, heedless of his knowledge; skillful in all professions, sensitive to artistic things; respecting intellectual or social supremacies, yet implying they were empty before the crucified One; equally indulgent toward others, while excessively rigorous toward himself; permitting the tyranny of the humble ones, though knowing how to make the despots obey; at home in a garret as in a palace; speaking to each his language; finally, as multivalent as life, whose abundances he admired—in all this, this man I mean remained ever-faithful to himself, as was his Master Christ, whose most unworthy servant he deemed himself to be.

The son of very poor peasants, the eldest of five, he was sent at an early age to the adjoining town, where he pursued quite advanced studies, all the while earning his living. Already in his native village he had performed miraculous healings with no means but prayer. In the large industrial center where he spent most of his life, the incurables, the destitute, and the desperate soon met this discreet benefactor, whose youthful wisdom restored to them the courage, health, and resignation so needful to the humble people whose obscure woes support the social edifice.

Besides healing, many other favors were asked of him: the success of an enterprise, the safety of a soldier, discovery of the solution to a technical problem, the enlightenment of a troubled soul. In return, he often exacted the condition that the seeker indemnify divine justice in part through giving alms, a reconciliation, abandonment of a lawsuit, or the adoption of orphans. Then, without fanfare, the miracle, the improbable, and the impossible would take place without anyone knowing how it happened. The only thing witnesses were able to know was that our mage condemned the practices of occultism as contrary to divine law, that he never employed them in any form, and that he did not recommend its theories.

His sole doctrine was the gospel. He appraised books according to their degree of concordance with this teaching. He proclaimed the divinity of Jesus, his universal sovereignty, and the perpetuity of his redemptive works. He accepted the accounts of the apostles to the letter, considering modern exegeses superfluous. He would say: "To the one who tries to love his neighbor as himself, heaven reveals the true meaning of the texts." His brief commentaries on the Holy Scriptures, to which he often added a new and living notion, had the singular property of answering at the same time the various interpretations given by independent thinkers and of conciliating the divergences of translators and commentators. Considering his contemporaries as unfortunately too smitten by intellectuality, believing the practice of virtue to be the only efficacious means of leading us to perfection, he did not waste words. He classified fraternal love as standing before all else—before prayer, even before faith. He used to say: "It is charity that engenders true faith and teaches us how to pray. Prayer without charity is easy, but faith without charity is not faith."

He counseled obedience to all laws (civil and ecclesiastical), regulations, and customs, so that by willingly giving "unjust Mammon" the gold and indignities he demands, our treasure in heaven becomes a reserve. He said "the meek of whom Jesus speaks are those who let everything be taken from them by the prince of this world, even the wages of their labor, even their lives. And it is in return for this deprivation that they will later possess the earth."

Above all, he condemned pride and selfishness; or rather, he did not condemn these faults, but pointed them out as the greatest obstacles to our advancement. He would say: "Heaven ignores the proud." "If you do not go to the meek or help the poor, how will angels be able to come to you?" "We must exert charity toward all forms of life, toward our equals, toward animals and plants; we must be charitable toward the adversity our neighbor rejects; toward the discoveries and inventions that you must distribute gratuitously, since you have received them gratuitously; toward the laws leveled against you, though you think them unjust, lest in rejecting them they fall upon your brother— for who, in truth, is your brother, if not you?"

This great practitioner of mysticism placed prayer after charitable works and inner discipline.

"You must pray and thank God ceaselessly. You must pray anywhere, at all times, because God is never far from you. It is you who stand apart from Him… You need only ask from the bottom of your heart, without scientific formulas, because even were you to look everywhere among the millions of worlds and suns sown by the hand of the Father, never would you find anything better than the Our Father prayer. If you dare not address our so kind Father directly, then pray to the Virgin, and she will present your petition to her Son, who will accept it." "However," he added, "for our voice to reach heaven, we must be very small. Heaven only heeds the weak."

These simple teachings, so pure, so direct; these strong and good words, both precise and full of the most grandiose poetry, hid (to the great surprise of some) a very concrete and, as it were, universal knowledge. This man, lacking higher diplomas or degrees, baffled specialists in all branches of knowledge. For example, I heard him call to mind some legislator's long-forgotten decrees, elucidate a text for paleographers, furnish an apparatus to physicists, indicate to botanists the locale where a rare plant could be found. Metaphysicians consulted him, as did both doctors and industrialists in matters of hazards. Statesmen and financiers sometimes followed his recommendations. He himself compounded medicaments, invented appliances and useful products. Indeed, he left no stone unturned in quest of improvements in applied science.

Yet neither his theoretical knowledge nor his technical expertise seemed to have been acquired by ordinary methods. The two or three intimate friends he invited into his laboratory have never revealed much about his findings. But certain words offer a clue to a few of the principles that inspired him. I quote a few of them gleaned over the years:

> A child of God—a being pure enough to sacrifice himself for any one of his brothers and then forget that sacrifice—can know everything without study. He can interrogate any creature, and that creature will answer him: a star will reveal its secrets, a stone in the wall will call out the name of the stonecutter who chiselled it, plants will explain their virtues, and on the face of men he will read their acts and thoughts. God invites us all

to share this privilege, on condition that we have patience and love for our fellowmen. [Or again]: Everything possesses thought, freedom, and responsibility in diverse measures. Everything is alive. Ideas, things, inventions, organs—all are individual creations, related to and influencing one another.

Among other examples, he often gave this one:

A philosopher pursues a metaphysical truth. It is an encounter, sometimes a struggle, sometimes a celestial dialogue, between one of those unrevealed genii of whom poets speak, and the human spirit temporarily inhabiting an earthly body and oppressed by the emanations of the unknown Presence. It is a cerebral reflection of such inaudible encounters (which we call intuition, inspiration, invention, hypothesis, imagination) that becomes then the nucleus around which the elements of a conceptual formulation, a mechanical invention, a more sublime art, a more profound doctrine, are organized by painful but patient effort. If we are blind to these spectacles it is because we do not believe them possible—out of pride, out of intellectual pusillanimity, and also because the Father does not want to complicate our task, or burden us with too heavy responsibilities.

If all branches of modern knowledge seemed familiar to this singular searcher, the most startling thing was that when I questioned him on several antique beliefs now considered superstitions, he answered at length and offered experiential proofs of their veracity. Long before our modern physicists, he taught the mass of light, the correspondences of colors with sounds, chromotherapy, the relativity of space and time (and the multiplicity of their forms), the complexity of simple bodies, the existence of unknown metals, and other peculiarities I will not now speak of, as they would seem far too improbable for positivistically inclined minds.

⊕

This Christian, this philanthropist, this scientist, was however, above all, the most extraordinary mage. I saw him accomplish all the marvels that saints such as Vincent Ferrier, Francis de Paul, Joseph de Cupertino, and the Curé d'Ars had operated, or those performed by strong wills that swayed crowds, such as Bernard of Clairvaux, Francis of Assisi, or Joan of Arc. Miracles blossomed under his feet. They seemed natural, infallible, and certain. Yet nothing provoked them but prayer.

A sceptic might call out: hypnotism! Oh no. Can a child with diphtheria, forty kilometers distant from the city where the healer lives, be hypnotized? No. Suggestion? No. Can cancerous, tubercular tissues be dispersed by auto-suggestion? Moreover, our Unknown condemned hypnotism, rural sorcery, and theoretical magic. He discouraged the use of any force of will or mediumship. Regarding mysterious powers that (we hear tell) certain sages acquire by means of methods going back millennia, he condemned them still more strongly—as leading straight to Antichrist.

No, for our Unknown it was a matter of simple, common prayer, such as Jesus teaches us. But whereas in the majority of cases, the saints obtain the gift of miracles after a protracted apprenticeship of extraordinary penance, prayers, and ecstasies, whereby their bodies become a field of physiologically inexplicable phenomena, our Mage lived in a simple way. He received his visitors any time, any place. And no sooner was the request formulated than he answered: "Heaven will grant you this," or "Go home, your patient is cured." His words were instantaneously realized. After which he would, if he could, escape from the gratitude of his debtors.

With no preparation whatsoever, he wielded the same power over animals, plants, events, and the elements. Several times he granted medical and scientific boards permission to verify his work. And these tests had a successful outcome. But one will search for such reports rendered by scientific academies and societies in vain, because none of the those conducting the relevant experiments dared sign their name to an account of such inexplicable feats.

Should I mention also his other, always spontaneous, unexpected, and benevolent gifts? The past, the future, and all of space were translucid to him. He would tell one of his consultants: "Your friend so and so is doing such a thing in such a place." Then to another: "On such a day, in such a year, you had such a thought." Further anecdotes I could relate so far surpass all likelihood that I prefer to stop here. Spiritually, a marvel is worth only as much as its author. Naturally, the gift of miracles interests crowds and leads quickly to fame, but it is the soul of the miracle, more than its form, that impassions the spirit of religious men.

I seek only to draw you to the soul of my hero and show it to you such as I had the privilege of experiencing it in my youth. It was superhuman, divine, like a star—yes, a star, daughter to the one that rose upon the terrestrial darkness twenty centuries ago. If after listening to me you still seek something else than heaven, then my story has proven useless and untimely.

To witness a miracle is not rare. To perform miracles, real ones, is not too difficult. But to think, love, suffer, dare, and will, according to the paths that remain constantly concordant with the eternal beams that end at the ministry of miracles—that is a superhuman task. In this sense, the miracle that comes from heaven constitutes a sign—the sign *par excellence.*

And here appears the tree of the cross, still a mystery after twenty centuries of study and adoration. Please understand that it was as natural for this man of whom I speak to cure typhoid as to pay a poor man's rent or to prescribe the exact formula for a reagent. All in him was paternal indulgence and inborn kindness. Everything about him was resourceful and tender exhortation, so that poor men and women could find courage and strength again, and receive some relief and solace. Just as a musician listens to nature, just as a painter observes nature, he—this remarkable Friend of God—lived in love and for love, because of love and by love.

⊕

He never spoke of this admirable flame within him. He hid both his knowledge and his (to some) disconcerting omnipotence under the cover of a very bourgeois life. He concealed his virtues and superiorities as we conceal our vices. You had to follow him on his long journeys through the populous suburbs to discover the excess of his generosities: desperate mothers watching for him on street corners, households by the dozen whose rent he paid, orphans whom he educated… And how kindly he treated the old and infirm, how delicately he offered financial help to timid and humble folk, how patient he was toward intruders, pretentious would-be pedants, and the ever-present flock of mediocrities!

And as much as our heart, barely human yet, can sense the secret motives of a heart so nobly superhuman, the innumerable gestures of his benevolence, his inexhaustible and always judicious beneficence, spring from a feeling that is incomprehensible to us: the conviction of his own insignificance. One day, a certain person who had asked a spiritual favor from this enigmatic personage (who moments before had cured an incurable) received this answer: "Why do you ask that of me? You know I am not even worth this stone upon which we walk." To all expressions of gratitude or admiration he answered with the same: "I am nothing. I can do nothing. It is heaven that does everything here."

Calling on him one day, I found him standing in his kitchen, lunching on a piece of bread with a glass of water. As I seemed surprised as his frugality, this man, who did not spare a moment for himself, who gave all he had, who spent his days and nights working, suffering for others, quietly answered: "I am having a wonderful lunch. Anyway, this bread God gives me. I have not even earned it." Never did he swerve from this unbelievably humble attitude. In this modern age of "everyone for himself," he stepped always to the back row, submitted to injustices, impatience, incivility. He played the role of voluntary dupe, smiling all the while, as though all unaware.

We read in ancient texts that sages rapt in contemplation of the serene splendors of the Absolute do not deign to take note of earthly events, and scorn the stings of the crowds' offenses. But the fact remains that rare are the philosophers who permit a bore to take their place in line! Minor foibles? Perhaps. But solid virtue demands more than accidental heroism. Do we not meet people capable of isolated heroic exploits who in reality are morally rather mean? And so, in accord with masters of the inner life, I believe perfection is not to be found in a few startling gestures, but in virtues patiently exerted day after day over a lifetime. Thus, the humble attitude of the mystic I speak of reveals the light to us better than his miracles and his teachings do. It is written: "Judge the tree by its fruits."

The sages I just mentioned illustrate a remote ideal always withdrawing behind cliffs or precipices. Their systems are always riddled with flaws. Their fervor, no matter how noble, is lost in abstractions. From their powerful hands life trickles away out like sand through the fingers of little child at the seashore. By contrast, with this man I speak of—so close to us all—we grasped all at once idealism and reality, theory and practice, the divine wedged into the terrestrial, the sum-total of which etched in us a most living image of what once upon a time must have been the living lessons of our Lord, Christ. There were no inconsistencies, no flaws, in the moral fiber of this perfect servant. He was always the same in nature, both stable and flexible—the profound harmony of which qualities made him unique.

The history of saints describes some as marvelous mages, great intellects, or flamboyant hearts; others as embodying a concern for the poor that leaves them no occasion for such soaring realizations. Then again, we read that there are some whose gift of miracles supersedes that of knowledge. But it is rare indeed to find all such gifts and splendors united in one, as in our hero. Even more rare is to find one whose powers manifest with such lack of effort. Yes, we find sublime theologians who meditate, and powerful soul-guides who watch and fast and weep. But the one of whom I speak healed in a commonplace manner, taught and consoled in a calm voice—and always with the same paternal smile.

I cannot adduce further evidence in support of these affirmations. I can only give you my testimony. Others have witnessed these same miracles, but they may have motives of their own for remaining silent. As for me, I have motives to reveal them. I cannot ask you to believe me. I ask only that you imagine them to be possible—that is sufficient. If accepting this as no more than an hypothesis one day makes you sensitive to the light, then my aim will have been achieved. I do not speak here in order to render justice to someone who cared so little about earthly justice. It is for you only that I speak—for your future, that you may find courage during times of stress and turmoil to take a further step forward, and then another.

⊕

This Frenchman, so similar to his compatriots and yet so very different, was of middle height and athletic build. Nothing in his clothes, manners, or language set him apart from the crowd. He lived like anyone else, except for the customary hours required for sleep, which he eliminated almost entirely. Married when quite young, he had had a son and a daughter. Though incessantly active, his body and brain never seemed fatigued. He was constantly occupied with chemical and mechanical research, with organizing social foundations run by friends, with social reforms that he submitted to the authorities, with inventions he gave to the needy. He was, in short, always benefiting others, though he did it secretly.

He did not much approve of lengthy discourse: no matter how complicated a consultation might be, he communicated his findings in a few packed sentences. He taught very little, excepting for some few suggestions given to humble and sincere seekers. He laid out no systematic doctrines; and yet, when added one to another, the seemingly unrelated lights shed by what he had to say to one who undertook to glean them patiently, finally formed a whole picture geared perfectly to that one's particular turn of mind, to their needs, to their professions. He taught individuals, providing them thereby all they might require to put together a system of their own, and yet he himself never promulgated a general synthesis of knowledge. Action interested him far more. He would often repeat: "If a man would love his neighbor as himself, that man would know all."

To such a being, the visible and invisible worlds vehicled a total realism where even abstractions are facts, where each moment of time is an actuality and all distances are present. Steadfast in the unfathomable yet living unity of which saints report having seen in their ecstasies but a few rapid flashes, this Friend of God was ceaselessly shedding upon all things and creatures the regenerating seeds of the spirit.

You are aware that from one century to another the eternal lamp is transmitted by the hallowed hands of the secret workers of the Father, who endeavor to fulfill the work of Christ. He, possessor of all magnificence, Lord of all creatures, having espoused all forms of abjection, placed himself at the bottom rung of temporal grandeur. Devoid of wealth, bereft of glory, without friends, he went so far as to give his mother to humankind—and from the abyss of such destitution he went forth to conquer the world. Each of his disciples must therefore reproduce one of the facets of his divine poverty, according to the darkness of the time in which the Spirit arouses it.

Yet in our time of progress, when the sick have their hospitals, the destitute their welfare checks, the orphans their orphanages; when slavery is officially abolished, when no one is really persecuted, because no one has too ingrained a conviction—in this time of ours, the image of poverty that our anonymous hero wore as a mask was that of being a nobody. A nothing. Not a pitiful beggar, someone hideously diseased, a celebrated philanthropist, a persecuted school administrator, a pursued escapee from justice; not at the top of the social ladder or on the lowest rung, but in the middle, at the neutral point. Someone "just like us" who in the public eye occupies the denuded, colorless stratum of mediocrity. Such was, for the nineteenth century, the admirable contrivance of divine mercy, since this insipid mediocrity will serve as an excuse on the last day for those who did not catch a glimpse of the light on account of the lamp being commonplace. Such was the subtle stratagem of divine wisdom, evading the curiosity of perverted minds thanks to the insignificance of the human form through which it operated. And one last word:

Jesus the poor is Jesus the patient. He suffers, submits, is resigned; he perseveres, obeys, and keeps silent. His friends, brothers, and heirs live without fanfare, lost among the multitudes for whom they have accepted to suffer, and who pay them no mind. The greater they are before God, the more they are misunderstood and the less they are known. So our century, in which nothing really can remain hidden, ignores this man about whom I speak, who held everything in his hands to sway the multitudes. Through the voice of a few renowned people, our century has calumniated, scoffed at, denigrated, the very man from whose hidden sufferings it profited. And this rescuer of so many shipwrecks never opened his mouth to defend himself, never permitted his followers to abash his persecutors, thus earning the right of repeating the divine request of the crucified One: "Father, forgive them, for they know not what they do." It is because I find in this Unknown a most perfect resemblance to Christ, the voluntary victim, that it seemed to me necessary to outline his physiognomy for you.

# The Master

AN'S ORDINARY PATH offers innumerable occasions for performing the tasks required of us. The good man who contents himself to follow that path faithfully merely has to rely upon and follow the dictates of his conscience and the orders of his Church, because there are also admirable people among materialists. Moral law is definitively impressed in each of us; and given that the first precept of any religion is altruism, any believer can find salvation in the faith into which he was born. But among the otherwise spiritually disposed, there are hardy minds and concerned intellects bored and wearied by the long, roundabout road. These seek elsewhere, throwing in their lot with various esotericisms and mysticisms, according to their intuition. It is to such spiritual adventurers as these that I dedicate the paragraphs to follow, in the hope that what I have to say will spare them from slipping into the snares of the wrong people, and from various pitfalls and quagmires.

To such seekers as these, who forswear the leaders of the large flocks, our very kind Father offers extraordinary instructors more suited to understanding their exceptional needs, more privy to the deserts and virgin forests of the invisible. How may one qualify for such a marvelous encounter? This is just what I will try to delineate in the course of a cursory survey of the great schools of initiation.

* First appeared in *Le Bréviaire Mystique*, and in *The Bulletin*, No. 7, January 1930.

⊕

The masters of *Chinese wisdom* (at the present time, the doctors of Taoism) pursue the conquest of self-knowledge (the "know thyself") only, even if their teaching entails some corollaries useful to social life. Very seldom do they make an exception and admit a foreigner to their school. In any case, after having provided the disciple with some primary principles, they abandon him to his own psychic and intellectual forces. By this I mean that if the student cannot advance on his own, this is taken as evidence that his capacity for knowledge has been reached. The implication is that no one can increase it for him, no one can offer him a helping hand to clear the obstacle. Moreover, were an "older brother" to hazard such an imprudent offering, the results (according to the masters of the Tao-tsang) would be as harmful for one as for the other.

The limited role of the Taoist initiator in any case ceases altogether once a student has reached a certain level of knowledge. Pure Taoism has no cult, no liturgy, and no sacerdotal functions. The student must first perfect his exoteric life-culture. Then, for the purpose of cultivating a contemplative psychic asceticism, he confines, or imprisons, himself in a "temple without doors." Finally, when he feels capable of going forth from that "temple," he leaves it, and, under his own responsibility, devotes himself to public teaching. He is responsible for his words, his writings, and his auditors. He may prefer to remain in such a gratifying role or he may elect to bury himself again in the confines of the secret colleges. However he proceeds, he has no other master than the abstraction of the Tao, which he will try to manifest within himself.

In short, as concerns the subject we are here addressing, we conclude that the mystic of the yellow race may count upon his self alone to perfect the triple impassibility, the triple equilibrium, the triple clarification—corporeal, psychic, intellectual—by means of which he hopes to assimilate the treasures of the past, to discover the celestial unknown of the future, and to ameliorate the physical modulations of the present.

⊕

The *Hindu*, no matter which of the innumerable sects of Brahmanism he may belong to, calls his method of salvation *yoga, union*. Among the eight forms of yoga, the highest is that by which the individualistic "I" is absorbed into the universal *Self*. This is *raja yoga*, the central branch of the *jnana yoga*, union by means of knowledge.

A second method is *bhakti yoga*, union by means of spiritual love. This love may be proven through religious practices. But if the devotee has only temporal advantages in view, he goes to hell after death for having profaned a holy feeling. If the devotee adores his god, if he chooses the greatest among the gods, if he loves him among his manifestations, he goes to a paradise after his death and is reborn a Brahman. Finally, if he loves with a pure heart, devoid of personal desires—as far even to the death of his self—he attains the Absolute.

There is, lastly, a third method, the yoga of action or work, *karma yoga*. Its focus is on action with the sole aim of fulfilling the law of the Absolute.

The first two yogas require the guidance of a master, or *guru*. The means for seeking out such a master is described as follows:

A first and indispensable prerequisite is that the disciple must have fulfilled the entirety of his family, civic, political, and religious duties—which necessitates an extended series of prior lives dedicated to *karma yoga*. Then he must create within himself four states of soul:

(1) Capacity to distinguish the relativity of the unreal from the absoluteness of the real;

(2) Renunciation forever of the visible and invisible fruits of his labors;

(3) Control of desires;
    Mastery over emotions;
    Abandonment of outer worship;
    Patience amid pain;
    Focused understanding;
    Steadfast faith.

The above accomplishments signify having achieved:

Control of the senses and extreme attention to
    perceived objects.
Control of the inner senses, directing them to them-
    selves, which provides perfect control of actions;
Reduction to nothing of all temporal preoccupations;
Desire for the light, despite all obstacles, with consum-
    ing ardor;
Unceasing tension towards the goal, through desire,
    study, and discussion;
Humility and respect for God, sacred books, and
    tradition;

(4) Above all, a desire for deliverance; a deep, ardent, dolorous, passionate aspiration. "Strive for salvation,"

says a guru, "as if you were trying to escape a fire; be anxious for success as the traveler is anxious who crosses a tiger-infested jungle, as he who passes near a den of thieves, as he who is poisoned and awaits the effects of the antidote he is made to take."

And these are no mere points of view or simple beliefs—they must be deeply graven in the soul. In the persevering disciple, these four qualifications must be like an integral part of his psychology: like second nature; like innate modes of his spiritual life.

When this titanic task has been accomplished—and no matter what temporal improbabilities supervene—the guru appears: the disciple knows then that the master has to come, and is not surprised at his sudden appearance.

There are *gurus* for each of the esotericisms: for knowledge of incantations, *guhyavidya*; for knowledge of sacrifices, *trividya* or *yajnavidya*; for ceremonial magic, *mahavidya*; again for knowledge of sacrifices; and finally, for mysticial union, *atmavidya* or *raja yoga*.

The god of the gurus is Shiva, under the form of the taciturn *Dakshinamurthi* because, says the woman-adept Avvaiyar: "Silence is at the limit or terminus of knowledge." The human master is thus free of time and space; in him, knowledge is veritable, the mental state is immobile, his heart immovable, his conduct kind. The disciple, the devotee, the indifferent, and the sinner all benefit from his presence. He has drained the dregs of his destiny; he has undergone all the consequences of his prior acts: voluntary as well as involuntary, or those done under duress.

Beyond the visible forms of objects, his mentality discerns the subjective universal form, Brahma (*dryyasanouviddha samadhi*); beyond the names of objects, beyond their cosmic elements and their specific differences, he discerns the identity of the self—as spectator of the world and non-actor (*sabdanouviddha* or *samprajnata samadhi*); he probes deeply into Brahma, sole reality, absolute certitude, fixed equilibrium (*nirvikalpa* or *asamprajnata samadhi*). This is the first stage of definitive emancipation; the Yogi may leave it at will temporarily when a disciple needs him.

His mental body, freed from the notion of the thinking self and freed from the notion of thought, does not recognize anything else than the thing thought of; the knowing subject, the object known and the organ of knowledge are unified (*amanaska, ounmani, samadhi*). Beyond that, there are but three more infused, transforming, and identifying ecstasies:

> Desires, intentions, and volitions have vanished into beatitude (*nissankalpa samadhi*);

> The notion of the essential elements of beings has vanished (*nirvrittika samadhi*);

> Impressions or innate ideas have vanished (*nirvasana samadhi*).

> Beyond is the inconceivable abyss of Nirvana.

⊕

Theoretically, the relationship between master and student was the same in Brahmanism as in the primitive, original *Buddhism*, which one does not find anymore today except in Upper Burma [Myanmar] or in Ceylon [Sri Lanka]. The differentiation between the two systems is found in their method of asceticism. Sakyamuni only established the rules and regulations concerning the general duties of laymen and monks. It was his disciples who codified his maxims.

The supreme master never appears anywhere as a god, or as God. He is, rather, a man whose knowledge and will have lifted him out of all gearwheels of time and boundaries of space—on earth, within our zodiacal sphere, in all cosmic systems. This superman, or rather that soul, whose loftiness attenuates into an abstract entity, resides nowhere and hence is present everywhere. This is why the compassionate one says of himself: "The one, however far from me, who still walks on the right path, is always close to me." And yet: "No man can save another."[1] Thus, "filled with love toward all things that are on earth, Gautama practices virtue for the benefit of mankind... his objective is to help innumerable beings without forgetting the lowest... Because his heart melts with pity, yet remains firm and steadfast as the steel of a spear," the soul who seeks him inevitably meets him. In fact, "the body may wear the garb of an ascetic, while the heart is concerned with worldly vanities; and the body may wear worldly finery, while the heart ascends very high toward heavenly things."

Thus it is that the Buddhist master, the venerable *Arhat*, "is he who, having penetrated into the essence of things, always aims at being useful to other creatures... any kind human words that reach the people are his words... Mediator for those who are divided, living encouragement for those who are united, peacemaker, friend of peace, impassioned for peace, bringing words of reconciliation, of understanding, triumphant over all adversaries through the force of his love"—this venerable one teaches his disciple through example and through speech that "it is better to die while fighting the tempter than to live beaten, subjected to him."

---

[1] The *Dhammapada*.

The Buddhist must first understand that nothing exists outside of man's thought. His moral code is based on the perfecting of thought—i.e., restricting it. This restriction is primarily physical, hence there can be no murder, theft, adultery, prevarications, or sensual pleasures; no asceticism either—in short, only constant equilibrium.

The Buddhist monk is a man who renounces the world totally, who follows a spiritual superior one-on-one, or as member of a community. The perfect superior, the *Arhat*, is the adept who will not be reborn after his present incarnation. He can take all forms, perceive all phenomena, all substances, all spirits, and all the prior modifications of creatures. Hence he knows his disciple's total individuality, and so can guide him in full knowledge of the facts.

The disciple must practice the eight branches of knowledge that comprise all physical and mental works: be it perfection in perception, reason, speech, action, life, effort, memory, and ecstasy.

He attains the perfection of physical works by means of observing the five abstentions mentioned above. He also attains the perfection of mental works by meditating upon a list of intellectual questions that varies from one century to another. In this way he acquires:

1. Sympathy towards the joys and pains of all creatures.
2. Aversion toward the body and everything connected with it.
3. Exact analysis of the phenomenal world.
4. Fixation of the mental body concentrated upon the subject to be studied.
5. Fixation of the mental faculties upon the essence of things.

As one can see, the role of the guru is reduced to guiding the disciple's moral faculties through a precise, programmatic routine, and sustaining his thought processes through an experience of the innumerable intellectual states.

Well, this is unquestionably quite a magnificent and captivating program. But let us be aware that it starts from a negation of life, since the Buddha lays down as a principle that the objective reality of the universe is an illusion of the self, that even the self is unreal, that everything may disappear into the void, and that "individuality does not exist, nor does non-individuality either." But, as someone else, Christ, has said, "The kingdom of my Father is eternal life." Let the reader make a choice.

⊕

Having risen by stages from the doctrine of non-acting, to the doctrine of non-thinking, to the doctrine of non-living—and thereby having come close to losing ourselves in metaphysical-mathematical abstraction—we turn now to *Islam* to bring us back to a vigorous notion of objective life.

The Muslim mystic, the Sufi, experiences an invisible world populated, like the visible world, with real creations, whose leader is the one Avicenna calls the Vigilant.

Man can attain direct perception of it with the help of the grace distributed to him by the saintly ancestors once favored with the same prerogative.

There are five degrees in the mystical hierarchy of Islam:

1. The faithful at large.
2. The three hundred.
3. The forty.
4. The *abdal*, all those who have replaced condemnable qualities by praiseworthy qualities.

5. The *pole*, the unique one, the one to whom the Father communicates Himself constantly, after having given him a secret, a talisman. This man travels in spirit through all nature, in its bodies and essences, just as the vital fire travels through the flesh it animates; he is the canal through whom the divine influx passes, and who distributes it to all beings. This man incarnates the angel *Izrafil* as vivifier of the world, the angel *Gabriel* as thinker, the angel *Michael* as assimilator, the angel *Azrael* as rejector of useless elements. This tradition traces Islam much further back in time than when Muhammad realized it, and has it endure far beyond the expected time when it will disappear with our planet. Thus, this tradition places Enoch as the first of these poles, and, so as to justify its previsions, affirms that Elijah is still alive on earth, and that El Khadir, the St George of the Eastern Christians, lives in the depths of the oceans until the day of the Last Judgment. One may be interested to compare this legend, if legend it be, with that of Western Christians regarding the immortality of St John the Evangelist, and with Rosicrucian traditions regarding these same personages.

The Muslim who wants to attain the glory of Sufism abandons his family and belongings. He journeys to all the sites of pilgrimage and follows the strict regimens of the various fraternities that direct them. Among these sanctuaries (which are almost always tombs), there is one in whose shade the saintly founder of the fraternity (or else its contemporary shaykh) transports him into the interior regions of ecstasy—this, then, is the one he must join, adhering to and following its meticulous exercises his whole life long.

Thus, sustained by the love of his master, he elevates himself by means of his own love. The fuels for this fire are poverty, mortifications, and the *dhikr*, similar to the ejaculatory prayer of the Catholics.

Starting from the world of the senses, the neophyte contemplative raises himself by turns to the inspired world of the *jinn*, to paradise, to the angelic world, to the world of the saints (where he finds his master again), to the world of the prophets, to the veritable world where Muhammad is enthroned. These seven planets comprise the 70,000 veils in which Allah, Light of Lights, the One, envelops Himself.

In the *aspirant* state, he has broken the bonds of secondary habits; entering the *path*, he devotes himself solely to spiritual worship, in the company of angels; acquiring the *truth*, he exercises the corresponding powers and gets rid of sinful possibilities; and finally, he reaches that *union* where only God and his servant remain, united but distinct.

⊕

Apart from these major religious schools there exists another path, a school of initiation that claims to unite the intellectual teachings of the ancient mysteries with the spiritual intuitions of the gospels. This school teaches and recognizes Jesus Christ as the Son of God incarnate, but denies the Church of Rome. It teaches all the ancient esoteric sciences, but only after the neophyte has reached perfect moral purity. Its members conceal their mystical achievements under the cloak of alchemy. It is they who, after having left traces of their power and wisdom at the origin of the great religious and social formations on earth, emancipated themselves in the seventeenth century under the name of *Rosicrucians*.

Here are the personal rules they have laid down to help us reach out to them:

1. Before undertaking any intellectual quest, meditate on the life of our Lord Jesus Christ.
2. Curb the thirst to know.
3. To know one's own heart is to walk towards God.
4. Defer action until all circumstances have been examined.
5. Study the gospel with simplicity.
6. End every temptation with a calm, unyielding refusal.
7. Glorify God with all our powers.
8. Polite honesty; no over-familiarity.
9. Immediately obey superiors.
10. Never a useless word.
11. Submission of our own will is peace.
12. Sickness and disease detach us from this world.
13. Physical and mental neglect breed temptation.
14. Close ears to gossip.
15. Through triple charity, fulfill all the law.
16. What fault in others is not in ourselves?
17. A monk's robe does not make a saint.
18. Suffering is purification, initiation, power.
19. Work inwardly, according to outer circumstances.
20. Unite silence and activity, from our arms to our hearts.
21. Let us see what we are, and repent.
22. The great unknown of Wisdom is the Cross.
23. Is there any temporal pleasure that lasts?
24. Blazing zeal, tireless patience, humble prayer.

What's more, you must live up to all your family, civic, and social duties. Children's education, hospitality, charity, domestic worship, the creation of refuges, workhouses, societies for the indigent, meeting places for simple enjoyment, educational centers and lectures—those who labor at such works are overlighted by the spirit of the Rosicrucians, who by degrees draw them toward it.

But what is this spirit, who are the true Rosicrucians? One should listen to Robert Fludd, who divulges the existence of nine colleges that are secretly linked and in possession of the antediluvian truth. Their headquarters are: in Attica, facing Mount Athos; to the north of the Persian Gulf, toward Tiruvanantapuram [southwestern India]; east of Lucknow [northern India]; in Lucania [southern Italy], Mecca, Fez, and Egypt. They manifest themselves either through their direct disciples, other remarkable men with whom they form temporary alliances, or in their own persons.

It is God Who teaches them personally through His Spirit. He grants them the gift of tongues, the power to heal without medicines, grand gestures or feats of the will; He grants them the wisdom of numbers and of dreams, the interpretation of hieroglyphics, the alchemical art; pneumatosophy, the deeper science of music, divination of the past and future of men, of countries, and of races; mysticism, the stewardship of earthly destinies, and the power to confer spiritual baptism.

Eckartshausen states that one may meet them especially in the vicinity of lakes. Their outward appearance is nondescript; their eyes have an unusual, startling, youthful quality; they may be of middle years, either single or family men, travelers or sedentaries. They acknowledge Jesus

Christ as the Word incarnate. They shun celebrity; their speech is simple and concise, but carries a secret virtue that touches hearts. They make themselves the servants of all; their munificence is inexhaustible, they radiate the light spontaneously.

⊕

From this short inquiry let us draw conclusions useful to us Westerners, Europeans, and Christians. Whoever is satisfied with walking the common road needs little other than his own conscience, secular wisdom, or ecclesiastical guides. But whoever wants to take the short-cut, the narrow path, runs terrible risks. Torrents, avalanches, vertigo, tempests, wild beasts, cold, brigands: the seven enemies coalesced against the mystical Thebaid that each one carries within himself.

Taoism, Brahmanism, Buddhism, and Sufism have one fault in common: they are methods of non-acting, evasions from life, negations. Before permitting any contemplative exercises, they point out that moral improvement is an indispensable requisite. They seem to forget that in life, the struggle between good and evil will only cease with the end of the world, and that if one were to attain the state of sainthood today, would it insure the identical state of sanctity tomorrow? Perhaps in the next hour one may succumb to strange, more insidious or more childish temptations. Hence, to await having attained permanent perfection before wanting to devote ourselves to others, is to delude ourselves. What is more, this training amounts to a kind of reversal of vital forces, a binding of free will, an etheric, mental, or psychic vampirism that, far from delivering, forges a new, more subtle and rigid chain.

Therefore a *guide* is indispensable. The guide must know the path in close detail, the climatic conditions in all of their variations, the country under all of its aspects. He will speak to the traveler in his mother tongue. The guide will not be a spirit, an elemental, or a god; it will be a man of flesh and bones whose gigantic spiritual stature has developed slowly over many centuries in the fulfillment of all of the Great Work. Sometimes at odds with the coalition of all the forces of darkness, he must be able to draw with his full hands on the Father's inexhaustible treasure. He must therefore be pure and free; his personal work must be finished. A master consequently an involute, a re-descended, a savior, a new incarnation of the Father's tenderness for his children; for as Balzac says, "To die for love is human, to live for love is heroism." In saying this, he confirms Swedenborg's maxims: "To speak is to sow" and "Where there is inner peace, there is God."

How does one meet that Unknown? Balzac replies again: "Knowledge seeks; love has already found."

And so, when your enemies oppress you, when your friends abandon you, when your children scorn you, when your bosses exploit you, when your ideal escapes you, when the whole of your strength, will power, and desire slackens, slows down, seems to vanish—have no fear: this is the first summons from the master whom without your knowledge has from his vantage-point seen you passing by in the valley, and from the radiant summit of the mystic mountain has elected you.

Be happy, then, in your agony; and begin to turn your soul's gaze towards the Unknown Friend. Your path bifurcates, and from this moment you will be on your way to bliss.

Do not seek for this master with your intellect—encumbered as it is by preconceived ideas, all tied up in systems, vacillating among the myriad broken images of permanent reality. Seek him instead with your heart, your poor bruised heart, your precious heart that angels cherish.

The moment is approaching when the master will appear before you. Whether in the filthy rags of a beggar or the regalia of a prince; whether as handsome as a seraphim or marked with the stigmata of fatigue, age, or martyrdom—never you mind! Do not challenge the outward appearance, listen to your heart—never before has it cried out so! The ravishment it experienced when it met the virgin-sister of your soul is nothing in face of the sovereign beatitude that engulfs it now. Your intellect falls inert, like an eagle blinded from having too closely faced the sun. The spirit of your bones groans, drunk with unbearable intoxication; your vital flame runs in all directions through your body, like an imprisoned mistress who sees her lover coming. Thus does your heart dash faster than lightning toward the heart of this Friend. Your heart hurries toward him. In him it loses itself, is transported with joy, finds itself, dies in him, then is reborn in him: blessed death, divine rapture, unquenchable thirst, profound peace.

But how many desolate nights before the crimson radiance of this dawn! Never mind! The constant, passionate, faithful seeker will see that resplendent dawn as soon as the shadows have become their most obscure, because it is written: "I come as like a thief in the night."

# Druidic Initiation

HE DRUIDIC INITIATION is remarkable in all respects. It contains the original or primitive forms of the light that were given the western peoples. It was especially formed, elaborated, built-up for particular qualities of intelligence, heart, and corporeal constitution of Europeans, of Celts. This initiation is healthy, true, and orthodox with respect to absolute truth—that is, as much as it is possible for any doctrine to be, other than the gospel itself.

We know only the outward doctrine of Druidism. Its secret initiation could not be found today, save by examining certain hieroglyphics inscribed on unhewn-stone monuments that officially accepted findings of archaeology claim to be far predate Druidism. A certain Brahmanic school in the vicinity of Faizabad possesses some of its keys, and the proportions of the Pyramids indicate a few others, for there have definitely been Celtic immigrations into those countries.

In the vicinity of the Boreal pole, about thirty thousand years ago, there fell a shower of rough stones from a neighboring planet. The length and abundance of these showers were deeply graven into the memory of the few savage hordes who became the ancestors of the Celtic race. And when a social state was organized, when priesthood and initiation were established, this legend became the foundation of the Druid cosmogony and androgeny.

The whole mystical organon of knowledge and power was based on four phases: (1) The rough, or unhewn, stone falls from heaven; it settles in the earth; it is seated and worked into the form of a cubic stone; it rises to heaven as a precious stone with one hundred and forty-four faces. (2) Stone-cutting is the work of initiates—a hidden, silent, mute work, which is why public monuments in Druidism as in primitive Judaism, in the Maghreb as in Afghanistan, are of rough stone. (3) The triangular or quadrangular pyramid is only a fraction of a cube. The round table is the projection, the earthly shadow, of the rising stone and its faces… (4) The soul of patriarchal Druidism is still alive. Deep, secret prehistoric connections link it to the doctrine of Christ.

# The Little Shepherd

nce upon a time there lived a poor young shepherd, seeming simple of mind. He watched over the flock of a village lost in the depths of the forest Brocéliande—in his day, thicker and wilder than in ours. This young shepherd, called Yann, did not know his parents. When very young he appeared in the village, whose simple, kind folk took him in. When old enough to find and follow the scantly-traced tracks wending through the woods, the village folk put him to the task of shepherding, among the hills, their little flock, which was all their fortune.

Yann lived an uncommon strange life. Seldom was he seen; barely was he noticed as he crossed the road at dawn blowing his horn, or in the evening bringing the flock to their stalls for the night. He spoke little and seemed often absent of mind. At night, instead of sleeping in the barns on their good fresh straw, or under the warming breath of the herd in winter, he would wander in the forest, craning his neck to the moon and stars. To the good village folk he seemed an enchanter.

Some had seen him amid the timber-trees giving ear to hidden voices and smiling at scenes they could not see. The forest seemed his teacher. He gauged the weather from patches of blue sky breaking through the forest's leafy crowns. He learned what herbs heal bruises, stanch wounds, or heal the herds. Even the crows and owls addressed him.

And when death visited this forgotten hamlet, he knew in advance at which hut it would pay its call.

Thus did Yann grow in happiness amid the fragrant forest airs. The flowers of summer, the fruits and golden fields of autumn, the winter's snowy carpet throws, had wheeled round many a time before ever he felt anything but admiration and peace. Among trees and herbs he counted none but friends, for never a one did he harm. He picked no fruit, pulled no root, cut no stalk, before asking leave of the plant his friend. Searching out sap-rich leaves for dressing wounds, never did he strip them from their stem without asking leave. He would amble first through the forest, raising his voice to inquire "Where might the St John's Wort be?" Or sometimes, with other herbs, he would inquire "Which among you will offer some few leaves to heal old Mary-Anne, or stanch the wound of Alain the carpenter?" Then might a small shrub make answer: "I will! Take what leaves you need, but do try not to hurt me."

And so, that he might not harm his forest friends, little Yann would wait till sleep fell upon them in the moonlight. Only when all these forest-children were peacefully asleep would he gather what leaves had been offered him, taking care to leave but faint marks upon them by sealing the green scar with the greatest care. So it was that all loved him and gave with pleasure what he asked.

Yann told the villagers of these woodland doings, and they wondered at his tale, for not one among them had heard the speaking of a shrub. When the little shepherd saw how they marveled, knowing nothing of the forest folk, he was much surprised. He was but a simple lad, respectful of elders, of no mind to be prideful of his woodland magics or to worry out their cause.

But still, as his kenning grew, marvel-upon-marvel, under the tutelage of his neighbor trees, Yann dared speak to the villagers of such things, thinking they would be a welcome benison; for just so had the trees responded when to them he told in turn the customs of the people. The trees paid Yann mind and profited from the tales he told of men, for they were humble, knowing full well that men were far above them.

But the peasants would say of Yann: "What a simpleton he is, fairies ever darting through his brain." They took no heed of his warnings and yes, paid dearly for their neglect. Trees, you know, feel a great many things that we men, even those closest to nature, cannot. They can tell what weather is on the way—not just a few days forward, but for many a coming moon. Indeed, the giants of the forest can espy these events years afore their time. The mysterious presences that fill many a traveler with fear beneath the vaulted, somber, green foliage are likewise within their ken. Those among them that grow along the skirts of the roundelay clearings where fairies dance on the sixth, thirteenth, twentieth, and twenty-seventh days of the moon, are the best informed. If we knew how to put questions to them and hearken to their answers, they would introduce to us the elementals of fields, brooks, waterfalls, rocks, ravines, and mountains. We would learn where lie useful soils and precious minerals; where the undines bestow medicinal virtues upon water-springs, and the flowers are balsamic. We would know which centenary oak has been blessed through the austerities of a hermit, which is haunted by the memory of a crime or the agonies of a suicide—and so many other things!

But, like civilized people and scholars, the worthy farmers among whom Yann lived paid no heed to his stories; they even laughed at them among themselves. Yes, white frost and hail did always come just as the little shepherd had foretold, but these lessons did not benefit them, for, to their mind, they were given by a vagabond who had fallen from who knows where.

Then one fine, sunny afternoon, while stepping through undergrowth carpeted with rampant ivy, Yann noticed that the ivy's leaves were not straight up to the sun's rays as they should have been, but instead lay edgewise to them. He knew at once that he had been drawn to this corner because something important was impending upon him—for one knows that ivy, which beholds the bad humors of animals, did not want to obey the law that day; and Yann felt cold at heart. He bedded down his cattle in the barn, then ran by moonlight toward the great oak Arra'ch, master of the forest.

But it was council night, and Arra'ch had gone off to the chief of the tree spirits for tasks to come, and to receive news from the mouth of the old bear, through whom spoke many of the elemental beings of this antique land. Only towards morning did Yann hear the voice of Arra'ch in his dream: "You are to suffer; and whatsoever else may come your way, you are growing up. You will have to choose between two roads, taste one of two fruits and discard the other. You must make the choice on your own. I can do nothing for you, as you are a man and your spirit is high above mine. Someday, if your spirit chooses wisely, it will be master of this forest. It will be my master as well, and master both of old bear and the gnome-spirits at work within the northward rocks. You have been good to us, though, and so we will we be good to you in turn. I pledge myself in the name of the forest entire to come to your aid, so long as you do not forget us." Then Yann heard the prodigious murmuration of the great trees, the shrubs and grasses, all plighting their troth in unison with Arra'ch to Yann… provided that Yann did not forget them.

It must be said forthwith that the little shepherd was now become a handsome blond youth, ramrod straight and vigorous as a sapling, and that his handsome figure did not pass by the young girls of the hamlet unremarked. Till now he had been insensible of their blushing faces; to him, they were but comrades, by happenstance less nimble and less daring than the boys.

Now, some days after he had observed the leaves of forest ivy arranged in the odd manner as already told, it fell out that a dark stranger came to the village, a girl with large, immobile eyes and long hair. As Yann caught sight of her, something trembled in his chest. His nostrils, accustomed to the pure fragrances of grasses and the blossoms of blanches-dames or lady-spirits-in-white, first felt the fevered odors of the flesh. In his anguish, he turned to his steady counselors—but on that night the forest held silent. Only master Arra'ch briefly spoke, saying: "Only a short while now, till you have to choose."

The dusky maiden addressed him—seeing as he dared not speak. She came from a nearby treeless place where folk lived wedged together in great stone buildings, not in huts. Their implements were a complicated affair, their everchanging dress a sight to see. That they might sleep, eat, and care for their bodies, a great paraphernalia was of need. And so, when the stranger saw no such things in Yann's village, she was astonished.

Yann told her of his life, his friends, his masters the trees and fairy guides—of their talks and foretellings. He wished the maiden friend would speak to them also, but their voices did not find her ear. Even had she heard the words, their meaning would not have opened, since her spirit hailed from elsewhere. Instead, she mocked Yann. And though he inhaled with delight the sweet breath of the dark-haired girl and her cloying thick perfume, her scoffing pained him. She would that he come live with her among the rich and powerful, and those she called scholars.

Now, Yann knew nothing of wealth; but, of what a scholar might be, he had some inkling. For he, too, hoped to learn of secret, obscure, far-distant things—not least the enigma he sensed hidden in the beauty of his friend. But he dared not quit his forest; he would lose so much thereby. And yet, he could not live, or so he thought, without her dark, caressing eyes and delicious perfume, without her beautiful form before him. Thus did he fret till suddenly one fateful day he took the hand of his temptress and left with her for foreign parts in search of wealth and knowledge.

He asked of her the secret that her ruby lips withheld, but she thrust him away, saying: "Bring me gold, and you will have the mystery of my beauty." When he had gold, he knew this mystery, drank it dry, then wearied of it; he knew it likewise in many another women, and wearied of it likewise.

Then he searched out the mysteries of knowledge. He grasped forgotten things aplenty, not least the languages of long-ago and the dreams of ancient sages; but never could he utter the "open sesame" to swing back the gateway to the mystery of knowledge.

Then one day, knowing now full well that this mystery

lay beyond his grasp, it dawned on him that he had grown old. His hands trembled; his hair had gone gray. And so he returned to his dear forest to take up again his life in the village of his youth. But he went unrecognized. He became again a poor shepherd, just as he had been so long ago.

By night, Yann wept over a life that now seemed wasted, that had gone all so quickly by. He wept over wealth, love, and knowledge, all unawares that these had been the very trials of which the old oak Arra'ch had warned him when he was still a lad. He wrestled in his mind till he knew surely there was a God—a God quite other than the God told of in the books of learned men. And before this God, he bowed low in humility.

At that very moment there came the great host of the spirits of the forest, of the waters, and of the earth, heralded by the spirits of the air. They rendered him homage, deferred to his spirit, and to him pledged their troth. But Yann told them: "Do not bow to me, but to Him Whom I feel living within me, to Him Who has led my soul through secret paths, and Who at long last offers me poverty of spirit, kindness, and love in place of the gold, pleasure, and knowledge I so long sought."

Such is the tale of little blond Yann, the foundling.

# The Faithful Dog

"Watch, for you know neither the day nor the hour."
(Matthew 15:13)

ERE YOU ARE, staunch loyal friend, panting with joy because you know we are going out and you will make yourself useful. Steady my son, yes, you are coming with me. Don't you worry, I'm taking you along. Though you are nothing but a dog, I am certain that during this long trip I will follow your example many times.

From this very threshold you are already beginning the untiring "amble" with which you will weave vigilant circles around me until late at night. You will spare yourself neither fatigue nor concern. You are not aware of where I am going, but as long as you are accompanying your master, your heart is glad.

As for myself, at the end of long excursions I will rest, contemplating—in the distant azure, from the top of great grassy plateaus—the eternal snows of the violet sea. When overcome by exhaustion, I will find relaxation in the fragrance of the orchards, in the curve of the undulating hills, in the gaiety of the villages. But you, kind dog, you will not permit yourself such respite. At the turn of a path, at adjoining bushes, your clear eyes seeking mine, barely will you permit yourself a few quick laps in the brook we are crossing, barely will you try to pick up the scent or trace the tracks of a recent passerby, because, galloping back, you will resume your encircling surveillance.

Faithful animal with powerful paws, in the evening you will sup on a few morsels and spend the night on the floor. I will care for you, remove the thorn from your valiant feet or the burrs from your fluffy coat. You will be grateful for my meager solicitude and sleep with one eye open and ears cocked, so as to defend me instantly—and if need be, perhaps die for me.

You, sweet kind dog, put me to shame, I who vaunt myself of belonging to the Master of Shepherds. How many more tender-hearted attentions does my Master shower me with than I ever give you! How unpretty is my surly laziness compared to your touching zeal!

I, who claim to bring back to the Only Shepherd the lost sheep and the docile ewes, how far I am from your zeal—you kind, loving dog with such soulful eyes! When will I disregard—as you do—fatigue, sleep, hunger, and thirst? When will I love hard work? When will I be able to inflame my indolence, to soften my mood and concentrate my dispersed forces? When will I be able to smile equally at indifference, ingratitude, and insults?

Yet, I know that what requires no exertion is worthless. The life of an idea requires that one suffer for it. And when that idea is Jesus, what ought not we sacrifice to his service? Nothing should appear too difficult. The hardships or difficulties we encounter earning our daily bread take the place at the end of the line. The struggle is nothing. Lack of success is nothing. Success is nothing. All that counts is the effusion of the effort from a heart liquefied by the flames of love.

I know all that. So why don't I move ahead? Also, it is too

late to change course; I am engaged, committed. Even if no one knew me as a servant of Christ, on the other side of the veil are brigades of creatures yearning for the light who are in anguish awaiting the living water, the uncreated source that is still enclosed within the rock of my heart.

"How long we must toil, always more work to do!" murmur some voices wearily. Does the dog ever weary of the tedious treks, as long as he feels of use to his master? Should we be less courageous serving our Lord Christ? Love is measured by the patience we exercise.

If we love Jesus, any advice becomes useless: pride, confidence, methods, energy, come out then as nothing but words employed by those who do not know how to love. To the one who dares because he loves, results are not important. There is always a result somewhere.

Let the sun shine within us. Let us smile at life. Let us welcome difficulties. They are the best, the strongest, mortar for building. They are precisely the tasks for which we are most qualified. Let us relieve our Jesus of having to take care of us, so that, at least once in a while, he might be able to rely upon us.

Let us be aware that the weight of this formidable hand on our shoulder for the duration of a single lightning bolt will bend us over and throw us to the ground. But you will get up. Bruised, but with indescribable joy of heart, you will get up—because in that ineffable moment you will know that you have been accepted among the faithful and tireless hounds of the Good Shepherd.

# Meditations Concerning Art

D O YOU BELIEVE that to form so fine a human being as a Pierre de Montereau, a Michelangelo, a Rabelais, a Bach, a Baudelaire, thirty or forty years would have sufficed nature? Who will fathom the depth of the prior paths of these souls, wending their way through lengthy, obscure, painful progressions? How many cloaks of life must they have worn in order that—in a few square feet of canvas, in two blocks of marble, in a hundred pages—they could amass and portray such varied experiences as still offer future generations the unfathomable wealth of their mysterious teaching? Please —do love geniuses, because they are the sublime bloom of their race, the savory fruit of a whole secular cycle; because they are martyrs and precursors; because all of them, even the most saturnine, reveal God to eyes avid to see God.

*Art* radiates a subtle life; it leads us more directly than does science or action toward immaterial glory. Or rather, it immediately sets aside the veils of the unrevealed—and that one glimpse suffices to enhance an entire lifetime. *Science* lets us discern upon these veils the shadows of angels and gods. *Action* in itself permits us (when we realize it in its fullness) to pass effectively to the other side of the veils. But it is *art* that incites in us the desire of ascending; it inebriates us to act, and gives us the ennobling melancholy of a feeling of exile.

Let us make our visit to a great work of art a solemn feast

by first preparing ourselves and collecting our thoughts in meditation. Let us bedeck ourselves with all we find within us that is noble and enlightening. Let everything be stilled as we take it in—let us become simple. Let it be for us a baptism of light and harmonies. Let us become saturated with its essence. Let every word be forgotten before the poem we listen to, let us repeat the verses as marvelous incantations. And let our eyes be filled as from a miraculous spectacle! There is something behind color, behind a sketch, behind plastic art or verbal cadences, a great deal more than their mental sense—and there lies their mystery. This is where the redeeming virtue of masterpieces lies. This is what makes them "chefs-d'oeuvre." This virtue is the image, the echo, and the prolongation of that state of the invisible which penetrates us through and through; of that unreal which is true reality; of that ineffable state which is perpetuated harmony. This presence, this reality, this harmony: they are forms of the Word—they *are* the Word; they are the expressions of our Jesus—they *are* our Jesus.

Do love all beautiful things; make yourself love them. Dig out and fan the flame of this noble love within yourselves until such time as your tears flow and your enthusiasm takes fire. Here, in this purified conflagration, you will temper your will-power.

Only then will true compassion for your brothers still mired in darkness be born within you. Visualize their blind groping, envision yourself in their place, and have pity on them. You are—they and you—limbs of the same great body bound together. May the acute sensation of their misery sting you to the quick and engender in you the desire of helping them.

# Odilon Redon: The Seer

N O ONE HAS YET interpreted Odilon Redon[1] for us, as did Péladan in his masterful interpretation of Leonardo; as did Élie Faure of Cézanne. I am not a painter, and know nothing about art criticism; but I do know that Redon touches me profoundly. Hence, these few lines do not claim to be anything else than impressions I felt at the retrospective collection of masterpieces exhibited at Barbazanges. Is it not also a duty to speak about an admirable man one admires, and about a work so full of edifying details?

Redon's work is diverse: it encompasses decorative compositions, tapestries, still-lifes, copies, mythological scenes, original themes, pastels, oils, watercolors, etchings, red chalks, charcoals, and lithographs. Within these meandering media, and the apparent disorder of his inspiring works, one finds the simple curve of a profound soul for whom all the splendors of the earth and humanity were platforms from which it launched itself toward the baffling magnificences of the invisible.

---

[1]  Odilon Redon was born in Bordeaux in 1840 and died in Paris in 1916. The exhibition of his works at the Barbazanges Gallery that Sédir mentions took place in 1923. Other retrospective exhibitions of his work took place at the Petit Palais in 1934, and at the Musée de l'Orangerie in the winter of 1956.

Is not the spiritually-minded public I am addressing—whose first orientation is knowledge, then altruism—somewhat forgetful of the beautiful? Is not beauty the glory of God, his immense luminous aureola, the harmonious splendor of his expressive gestures, to which we may add the superabundance with which his beneficence embellishes all the acts of his power? Beauty—visible expression of the spirit—confers the marvelous gift of moving the beings she settles upon. But in elevating and projecting them far ahead of the crowd, she isolates them.

How long did Giotto, Leonardo, and Rembrandt have to wait until the élite was able to catch up with them? In our days, Henri Cros was so hounded by bad luck that even at the Luxembourg Gardens his admirable fountain was placed at the only spot where no one can see it. Auguste Lauzet, as universal an artist in technique as he is in thought, remains totally unknown because death overtook him at age thirty-three. Finally, there is Odilon Redon, who had a full career, but whom too few admirers have yet acclaimed. Cros is all about antiquity infused into a modern soul; Lauzet is all about nature and the divine humanized; Redon is all about the invisible, the incarnation of our dreams.

In art, the greatness of genius is never perceived by the crowd. A genius walks alone, far ahead—he is the spirit-adventurer. The "successful" artist rises but a small degree above the common course, preceding his epoch by a few steps only. He is "accessible," everyone can touch him if only they stretch out their hand. The genius, on the contrary, runs ahead, seems lost; but then, all of a sudden, in the distance, the piercing gleam of his torch shines out—for he paints the unknown, expresses the inexpressible, modulates for our ears the symphonies of the unsounding. Thus, he remains doomed to incomprehension. The public is willing to take up any teaching that is logical, practical, or rational; but no one can make the public overreach itself in the realms of taste, of sensitivity, of spiritual depth—such developments require centuries. And if a genius happens to be a prophet as well, it is true also that no man is a prophet in his country.

Odilon Redon so far has been understood only by a narrow circle. For a long time still, as it seems to me, he will remain unique, singular. His eyes perceive something beyond what other painters see. Through the simplest lines, his hand knows how to suggest the richest forms. He represents natural objects as translucid, supernatural. He presents to us spaces unknown to the geometrician, yet possible nonetheless, and creatures no naturalist has ever seen, yet given form by a most credible living logic. Moreover, he is master of his palette and of his lines at that supreme level of simplicity one calls style. Finally, he is a powerful transfigurer, who sublimizes into figures of eternity the passing beings whose fugitive appearances are reflected into our eyes. He surpasses the art of painting by reaching the essence of art, and that by a simple method: "My most productive regimen, most essential for my expansion," he told us, "has been to copy what is real by reproducing very carefully any object of visible, external nature, representing it down to its tiniest, most particular, and accidental details. And then, having first made this effort to minutely copy a stone, a blade of grass, a hand, a profile, or any other living thing from life, something mentally ebullient surges within me—I feel I must create, let myself go to represent the visionary imagery. Nature, 'dosed' in this fashion, inspires me, becomes my source, my leavening, my ferment."

"To put the light of spirituality into the simplest, humblest endeavors"—that he was able to do, because his soul was healthy and vigorous. As in the case of Puvis de Chavannes, the silent nobility and austere discipline of his private life have endowed his public works with a solid foundation and immovable framework—a secret our artists too often forget, those who, especially and above all others, should heed it. How many eloquent pages have been written on the need of artists for passion! Of course! Only ardent souls may express the beautiful. But what heights they could reach, what grandeur, what purity they could attain, were they to become masters of their passion rather than its slaves! Man is a compact whole: the most banal chink in his self-control reverberates within his soul and tarnishes it.

That is why, among integral human beings such as Odilon Redon, an admirable continuity unfurls in a double curve of equilibrium: out of their attentive regard, the exact vision of the objects thus observed ascends to the sacred surgings that invite inspiration, and from the spiritual heavens where archetypes hover brings them back to the pliant fingers under whose delicate touch a simple line becomes a high-relief that bathes and espouses them with depth, relief, and spatial air.

Fruits and flowers seen through such eyes are no mere pretexts for a magnificent palette. Rather, their hidden life breathes, and their spiritual force speaks. They are no longer roses of France, rustic red poppies, lemons from the Midi, or pomegranates. They are the flower, the fruit, the masterpiece of the realm of plants, the consummation of a myriad of obscure, forgotten efforts. They are the Garden, the Field, the Orchard. They are poems complete, small worlds, syntheses, horticultural stars.

Odilon Redon, aristocrat of form and color, this painter of ours, when he revives certain classical scenes from mythology, follows the grand circular march from the visible to the invisible. He is obsessed by Apollo and his rearing steeds in the startling magnificence of an aurora borealis. He depicts Andromeda or the beauteous Angélique with their liberators against the most subtle backgrounds that any primitives could have conceived, acting in concert with Le Lorrain, Corot, and Claude Monet—all of whom are recognizable in the trees, the rocks, and the mists of Redon. Under his brush the cold, secret symbols of the ancient East become living flowers, harmonious polychromes, scenes of pathos. The Buddha, Christ, Orpheus, the Holy Family, St George and St Sebastian, martyrs, women, angels—all such suprahuman beings have effectively descended upon his soul, and it is their taciturn visitations which in truth have guided his conscientious fingers.

What titles he gave his imaginative works! *The Knight, The Flame, The Lost Angel, The Fallen Angel, The Meditative Angel, The Martyr, The Flower of the Swamp, The Drowned Glory, The Astral Idol, The Wing*—and no doubt many more such prodigious theurgies besides, confined and hidden by unknown collectors! Here are some spiritual brothers of our seer, to whom fantastic theogonies have likewise imparted their secrets: Byron, Alfred de Vigny, Poe, Baudelaire, Villiers de l'Isle-Adam, and Mallarmé.

Odilon Redon converses with the ancient gods. He grasps the impalpable; he interprets the aura of the faces that fill our dreams. He navigates upon the ethereal rivers and confronts the formidable genii who pour out to exceptional souls the terrible wine of ecstasy. Never do his eyes falter, his fingers tremble, or his good taste wander. Such is the seal of genius: to keep within bounds all expressions of what is extraordinary; to employ verisimilitude in portraying the impossible; in short, to raise up the viewer to the realms of the unreal, and then deposit him again upon earth with such mastery that his dazzlement, far from arresting his desire for life, fans it to a blazing point of flame according to the law of perceived splendors—in this way forever bringing to a fine temper his yearning for nobility, intelligence, and love.

It seems to me that this is what the works of Odilon Redon tell the sincere visitor, the avid soul, the budding energy of one in quest of a path. The teaching of this modest master corresponds, in the spiritual order, to that of Giotto in the religious order, to Michelangelo in the animic order, to that of da Vinci in the intellectual order. Let us be thankful that France was elected to engender such an initiator, and let us become students worthy of his sufferings and of his hidden achievements.

# Contrasts

I HAD GONE UP to the golf course of Mont Agel above La Turbie. So splendid was the weather that we were ashamed of enjoying it, full knowing that millions are laboring in mines, factories, workshops, and offices, and that our dear comrades are trudging through the muddy dreariness of Paris.

The road traverses such beautiful bare hills, made up from thick high walls of white marble whose superimposed strata seem to serve as foundations to Cyclopean palaces.

For centuries, that indefatigable alchemist the sun has tinged them with its golden hue and infused them with its magnificent life. These stones speak to the soul. One feels whence come the influences they embody. They teach us lessons of perseverance and immutability. They lift hearts from peak to peak, higher than the hills where angels walk, to the very end of the shining path that leads creatures to the living center of the world, to the immutable rock whose adamantine texture remains indispensable to the solidity of human works.

In the distance, here and there, legions of standing stones recall the fall of meteors as told in ancient cosmogonies. Muleteers' trails zigzag across the slopes, testifying to the industrious effort of our ancestors: their obstinacy, their uncounted exertions, their worries—the whole doleful canvas of these humble peasant lives upon the living matrix from which arises periodically the splendid blossom of a man of genius.

Here and there, with melancholic pride, noble cypresses stand guard over long-gone portals of abandoned ancient domains. In the distance, toward Italy, ripple the shores of Cap-Martin, of Menton, of Bordighera. Toward the west, the peninsula of Cap-Ferrat bearing Saint-Hospice, the old chapel of the Templars, the promontories of Antibes and of Cannes. The spurs of the Esterel sink magnificently toward the golden mists of the sea. Before us, the rock of Monaco stands out like an immense ship upon the blue waters.

Toward the north the great plateau of the golf course unrolls its long, verdant, undulating grounds. From that point of vantage one descries the vast, confused mass of the dark, tormented Black Alps: somber rocks, gorges, forests; but beyond and above them, against the deep blue of the sky, glitter the dazzling fringes of the eternal snows. Because all depths, those of the sea as well as of the land, soar forth to the heights in one invincible vitality, offering man, for the instruction of his soul, the noble purity of whiteness—foam of the waves, glaciers of the summits, starry pearls of the firmament—they, all three, are beyond us, the triple repercussion of the wonders that our spiritual efforts sublimize within us.

Lofty horizons—similar to the fields where the bodies of the *gibborim* (the "mighty ones"), builders of the earth, would find rest—majesty of the wide-open spaces where, with the pure air wafting down from the snows, one drinks in a deeply refreshing, invigorating peace. Summits as bare as those where St John of the Cross experienced his ecstasies. Tiny villages suspended in the far-distant, shady valleys, like fixed swirls, eddies, frozen vortices, to the receding limits of the empyrean, temple of beauty, house of God—minus walls, minus roof—as vast as He who fills it with His ineffable Presence. Thou art there, most kind Father, and thou, Christ of the abyssal gaze, and thou, Holy Spirit, who fills it with all splendor.

But, where are your children—humankind?

Oh, here they are, at the grandstand of the dove-shoot. The most elegant of society hasten to remind the stroller-by that man is cruel and dumb, that wherever nature deploys her imposing handiwork, his first gesture is to soil it with some useless killing, and his vanity.

I thought of you, my friends, faithful servants of Christ, as I hearkened to this discordant note. How urgently your work is needed! How necessary, how impassioned, it must be—for the work of God is universal harmony. Within us, sublime landscapes unfold. You have seen them. Do you not nourish the desire of conserving the intimate concord between our energies and our great desires? You have discovered within yourselves immense fertile plains, peaks, immutable crags, and fresh water-springs. Remember that you must open the eyes of your brothers to these halcyon scenes.

Become poets of action, artists of spirituality, magicians of eternity. Cultivate the spiritual body, as the Greeks did the physical: cleanse it, exercise it toward noble attitudes, raise yourselves above your level. Do not be afraid to lose your footing; let yourself faint beneath the diamond breaths of the mystic snows, and in the midst of these transports turn towards these brothers beside you, and yet so far from you, so sophisticated and strong with the wisdom of the earth, yet killing doves for sport.[1]

---

[1] Since 1953, Princess Grace has forbidden these dove-shoots.

For sport! That means to escape from themselves. "We are not doing anything wrong," they say. They are cruel and stupid only because they are cowards; they are merely afraid of themselves; they dare not face themselves.

You who have heard the echo of divine voices, go towards them with the assurance that celestial kindness and human compassion grant you. Make it so, that they face themselves. Most often, they will throw you out. But go back. Your eyes, which, unknown to you, have been filled with the light that the sun of spirits grants, will serve as eloquent exhortations if they will not hearken to your voice. Thus you will have made good use of a little of what the Father has permitted you to perceive. This is one of the works of the precursor, John the Baptist. Another follows.

Between the motionless immensity of the sea and the immense immobility of the mountains, a second lesson awaited me.

The lunar crescent was already visible over the ancient tower of Philippe Auguste. The setting sun was nearing the horizon, already tinting the high rocky cliffs with dusty golds, muted pinks, and faded chrome-yellow tones. In the distance, the Italian mountains were sloping into the sea in deep lavender-wash tints, their elegant profiles reminiscent of Virgil's strophes. At my feet, over the dimming azure of the waters, projected a wild and barren promontory, a vast amber-colored field of ruins, a mass of broken stones, at whose extremity stood two Roman columns. This promontory is named "The Hill of Justice." There, once upon a time, stood a sort of fortress, where all the malefactors and criminals of the land around were imprisoned or hung. Before the time of feudal brigandage, the Roman road passed through there, in the center of a strategic town.

But what archaeologists are unaware of, and what you disciples of Christ must know, and what I was seeing at this very moment with such intense emotion, was a scene that took its course in this same prison almost two thousand years ago.

On a certain evening, a stately, tall traveler arrived on foot, making his way down the main street of this village. He was not a Roman. His hair was long and his beard short. At first sight, nothing distinguished him from other men. It took close attention to discover in his features the emanation of a superhuman power, and the mystery in his eyes. The stranger was tired. He asked for bread, figs, and shelter for the night. Accommodation had been made for him, when all of a sudden he presumed to defend a thief just then being led back to the fort after suffering the brutalities of the sergeants. On this account, the traveler was immediately apprehended, just as cruelly maltreated, and himself taken to the fort.

The singular aspect of this scene is that, despite his athletic stature and noble bearing, the stranger did not defend himself from these crude soldiers.

The next day they threw him out, and without a word the mysterious traveler continued his trip westward toward Marseilles and the Provence. Only a week later an earthquake unexpectedly destroyed the houses, the fort, and the temples of that village, and from that time forward, this hill remains of sinister repute.

Three kilometers further on, the mysterious solitary man received hospitality at the bottom of a vale on the road to Nice. It is there, fifteen centuries later, that the sons of the "little" Brother Francis of Assisi erected a chapel to Notre-Dame de Laghet.

Do you see, my dear friends, the hidden root of the brig-andage and piracy in which the fishermen of this coast for so many centuries excelled? Do you see this root shooting its venomous flowers into this casino, where all the greedi-ness and corruptions throng? Countries have their own des-tiny, just as we do; physical beauty is rarely in accordance with its interior beauty.

Here, then, is the second work of the John the Baptist. Let us try to establish a durable accord between the outer and the inner. We may establish this accord by means of sincerity. Only at that price will we establish within us the unified accord without which there is neither asceticism nor power. Only at that price will we become sowers of fer-vent ardor. Hard work, my friends, and a long road ahead. One that we must now undertake. Let us open the eyes of our spirit. Let us not be as those Romans of yore. We must come to recognize the envoy from above, no matter under what guise he shows himself. Has he not himself said that each beggar is himself? What a saying! How it increases our responsibility. How it enlightens, illumines us! Treasure that saying, make it your sword and your shield. Then throw yourself heart and soul into the thick of the battle.

These very paradoxes of which I mildly speak were the very ones John the Baptist cried out with the full power of his formidable voice into all the depths, upon all the heights, in all deserts, to all multitudes.

Remember his eloquence.

# Journal of a Trip to Lyon
# and Some Italian Cities

HAT A PLEASURE it was to return to that old city Lyons, which seems to me the grotto of the mysteries of France. Though so dark and sooty now, the old monuments laid out along noble, austere, somewhat emphatic lines, remain genial still. In the Croix-Rousse sector, the old houses with vaulted arches, multiple stairways, and passages with their fume-greased walls and doors revealing dark recesses (such as one finds in etchings) conserve an outworn, antiquated charm. Their inhabitants, as one can observe in the robust bone-structure of their solid old bodies, have come down perhaps ten aeons or centuries ago from high mountain regions or sun-drenched lands. Once upon a time they had perhaps been hardy Savoyards, cunning hard-drinking Dauphinois, vintners from Beaujolais. Now they are dark-clad troglodytes, all corrugated and wrinkled. Their stratified faces resemble hollowed-out rocks encroached upon by pale moss. Their speech maintains the sing-song tones native to their mountain villages, though their voices are now subdued. They are polite, philosophical; but beneath that calm, how much curiosity, disquiet, restlessness, and suppressed envy one feels! Lurking beneath the old arched doorways, beneath the ancient vaults, in the mossy court-yards, in the alcoves of their dank lodgings, they spy, ferret, grumble, bewail, slander—and yet happy in the belief they are leading wretched lives.

Tuesday evening, after dining in the pleasant large brasserie installed downstairs from the beautiful concert hall recently built at the foot of the Croix-Rousse, our friends the Georgets took the three of us to the Grand Café Bellecour. For me, these were three instructive hours. Lyon is a city abundant with music lovers; the music devotees bring to their enjoyment of good players the same scrupulous gravity, the same passionate, earnest, ingrained good taste they bring to all matters. Among the audience, few young men are to be found; one sees mostly mature and old men with rather plain yet strong physiognomies. They are cheaply clad, but are attentive listeners, indifferent to their neighbors.

The performance took place on the platform. There was an excellent German pianist, though perhaps a bit too self-satisfied; an albino cellist, an expert virtuoso; and a violinist, a dark-haired, bearded, pale-faced man, thin, nervous, passionate—and how wonderful he became when the Wagnerian daimon possessed him! How proudly he performed a Brahms scherzo! How tenderly he caressed the leitmotif of a Corelli! And how transported with religious fervor he became as his long saturnian fingers developed the pathos of a Beethoven adagio! It is good to find once in a while a man who has such fire in his heart—it warms and reconciles us to life!

⊕

We are leaving for Milano. After the nightmarish Simplon tunnel, the noble horizons of Lake Maggiore come into view. And now Milan. Streets paved with large granite slabs;

one dines late; men assemble, loafing under the arcades; lots of street cars; very correct officers; obsequious servants; window screens. Silent old hotels, beautiful gardens caught sight of through the porticoes. Lunch at Cova's.

Santa Maria-delle-Grazie: charming cloisters, beautifully toned bricks; what majesty in the outlines of the Last Supper which, although the fresco is almost obliterated now, still projects into the room the emotion of a powerful mystery. That, is genius.

At la Bréra: the cartoon of the School of Athens, more beautiful than the fresco; sketches of Leonardo's.

Wealth of the Palace Peldo-Pezzoli; admirable Luinis, the Christ of Andrea Solario; beauty, splendors, resplendence.

If we were to set Catholic painters to one side, on the other side we would find an essentially human artist, the Beethoven of the plastic art: Michelangelo; while further away stands the sphinx of the Renaissance: Leonardo da Vinci. This mysterious being seems to have known and understood everything. It has taken us three centuries to recognize this. The angel who guided his hand seems to have been a spirit of ancient wisdoms. At times, this spirit has the large convex forehead of the omniscient Rishis; he also has the undulating, androgynous body of the young initiates who once upon a time brought to man the lunar secrets of divine union. He smiles with the well-informed, conscious forbearance of a Gautama Buddha. Beneath a puerile form, his eyes recall the past; beneath a warrior form, he combats furor, luxuriance, and pomp, but with a peaceful heart. The outlines of Leonardo's portraits are bathed in, and palpitate from, his halo. When representing the Virgin, he reveals in the pure, candid young girl the superhuman quality of the divine Spouse, the inexhaustible mystery of eternal nature, effortless power, innocence, and science—nature as both good and evil. Finally, when he portrays Christ, this bearer of the Holy Spirit graphically represents via the hand of master Leonardo our universal Jesus—not the one of a church, but the friend of all humanities, the doctor of all the worlds, the chief, the center, the principle, and the end—the enigma.

⊕

Now on toward Genoa. Once past Novi, as sumptuous clouds darken the sky, the delightful hills we have just crossed change into austere, rugged, windy, narrow passes of the Appenines, where torrents flow over the jagged stones of La Serivia.

At Genoa's port, people mill about beneath the pungent, reeking arcades; many trattorias installed on the ground floor of ancient palaces have electricity; narrow alleys with rags flying; we see adolescents holding hands, kissing each other.

Refugees in the port. Spanish-Arabian architecture prevails; holy pictures everywhere; protruding pot-bellied balconies; bars on all the windows.

Regarding the ridiculous monuments of the modern Camposanto, the less said the better!

⊕

The Riviera of the Levant. Parasol-shaped firs; cacti, giant oleanders, corn; noble cypresses serving as windbreaks protecting the olive groves from the Levanters. After Nervi, the coastline becomes as barren as that of Brittany; old chateaux here and there, ancient watchtowers in ruins. A swarthy little girl wearing a red shirt goes by.

⊕

Pisa is irresistibly seductive to any melancholic traveler. We note the calm, noble Arno with its quays; the facades of ancient palazzi bordering all its streets on both sides; its poverty-stricken population, most of whom walk barefoot. We see the triple marvel of the Baptistery, the Duomo, and the Camposanto offering itself in silence, as a maiden from the East; the fortress, enceinte, with its old battlemented walls—all together exudes a perfidious narcotic charm.

Pisa is an elderly patrician lady who has known, heard, and seen everything but still enjoys mild flirtations; when the partner is subtle, he enjoys the wrinkles, the provocative smiles, the quaint gestures, the stiff pleats of her embroidered skirts. This Marchesa has given herself so much and to so many handsome lovers, that only the feigned preparations to love interests her today. Her lover knows it, and, should he possess her, it will be in the propitious darkness of the gardens at night, or in the obscure vastness of her tapestried bed chambers by candlelight. Such is the aristocratic Pisa—that is what the impregnable pot-bellied grills she fastens at the windows of her palaces and the grillworks with which she forbids entrance to her inner gardens represent; the comical silhouette of an old lady hastening to church, the lethargic Pisanine bearing of her gentlemen-in-white.

The proletarian Pisa is far more horrible; it is like a vision of Orcagna's.[1] Half of its common people are either one-eyed or blind; and what shocking examples of blindness!

---

[1] Andréa di Cione Arcagnola, also known as Orcagna, Florentine painter, 1308–1369.

All kind of viscous tumors on the eyelids, festering sores, all sorts of swollen, hollowed-out sockets, bloody, black, yellow, and oozing. Toward noon one witnesses the procession of these invalids coming out of the hospitals, their faces covered with bandages and cotton; and all of this horde of men, women, and children, scarcely clothed with dirty rags, are begging alms; they moan, and hate you—beneath the splendor of a blue sky.

But there is a third Pisa; this one wears a cloak of eternity; she is serene, suave, heart-rending. It is the Pisa of marble and color—witnesses of her ancient splendors. Nothing remains of what she had been twenty-two centuries ago; nothing remains of what she was from the year 1100 to 1400, but for her architectural jewels. One is a precious marble reliquary, so small that it does not disturb the passerby in the Gambacorti: the Santa Maria della Spina, a cut-work chapel worthy of a goldsmith's art, where the Pisan sailors, before leaving for long ocean voyages, would come to ask for the protection of the Queen of the Seas, and upon returning pay her homage.

In the corner of a square filled with enormous plane trees we find Santa Caterina with the tiered colonnades of her Gothic facade; here is her brother San Francesco; there her Romanesque elders St Frediano and St Pierino. Here again, the edifices of knowledge where Galileo taught, where in the sixteenth century more than a thousand students still thronged around sixty professors; and how many other churches, how many depopulated convents, and so many moribund palaces! How instructive is your antiquated beauty, how eloquent your silence! But the sons of this old mother do not comprehend her any more; the initiatrix of Florence has been agonizing for the past five centuries; she is well aware of it, and from her resignation reshapes and regains her nobility.

This decrepit ancestress has a smile of her own: the river Arno. She also possesses her own diadem: the square of the Duomo. One must come here in the morning when the bells of the peasants' teams have stopped their clanging and the inhabitants have not yet come out. One should in a single glance survey this quadrilateral of houses with flat brownish facades, the grassy soil split by stone walks, this exquisitely blue sky against which the leaning bell tower stands awry, and take note of a Romanesque basilica and a baptistry—immutable structures of marble, colonnades, and arcades. Solemnly they stand, white, inalterable, in a superhuman serenity which they communicate to humans; they represent the wealth, the effort, the courage, the faith of a people. Their beauty expresses the outpouring of the soul of a staunch, solid city. Yet they are nothing but heralds, because, back of them, slumbers the marvel of marvels.

Behind a long white wall crested with reddish-brown tiles, as is customary in this land, is a little door through which you step into the Camposanto. You find yourself in a kind of one-storied cloister, whose length is two-and-a-half times its width. The curved part of the arches are semi-circular, with very simple moldings. In the grassy courtyard, two cypresses stand watch over a capital, the font-head of two ancient fountains, and four shrubs. On the walls, two faded figures are still visible. And that is all—such is the masterpiece of Giovanni Pisano.

The perfect harmony of its proportions, the simplicity of its decor, the tombstones upon which one steps, the silence reigning within this august enclosure—all of this brings an inner stillness that restores peace within us. It takes us out of this century; it facilitates reading and interpreting the great mysteries that Orcagna, Gozzoli, Giotto and their students have painted upon its murals.

Didactically, for this study, we must start with the north wall, proceed to the west, to the south, and end with the east wall.

The north wall retraces the entire Old Testament. The eight subjects on the upper part are done by Pietro di Puccio. Seventy years later, from 1459 to 1485, Benozzo Gozzoli painted twenty-four subjects at the bottom, from Noah's inebriation to the queen of Sheba. Though he was Botticelli's contemporary, he could be his master, because of the vigor, firmness of the lines, compositional arrangement, and sobriety of that charm which, in the works of the painter of the "Primavera," occasionally overflows to the point of causing one to overlook some negligences in rendition and inadequacies in composition.

The west wall designs are almost obliterated now.

The south wall depicts the triumph of death. Whether it was painted by San Traini or Andrea Orcagna, whether Job was depicted by Fra de Volterre and not by Giotto, whether the painters of the hermits of the Thebaid, of San Renier and others, be known or unknown matters not, since these venerable teachers did not even care to sign their works. This is the first lesson they give us, the greatest perhaps—in any case, the one that can be best understood by the greatest number of people.

The east wall comprises the events in the life of Christ that have some association with death: the crucifixion, the ascension, the doubting of St Thomas, the resurrection. It is believed that these frescoes were painted by an anonymous successor of Giotto.

Everything has been said regarding the freshness, the grace, the candor, the nobility of these paintings; it is in the details that what is "real" is to be found. Meanwhile, idealism brightens up their harmonious whole. Being a mere amateur of painting, I can perceive only the soul quality of these artists: such a definite love of life, a vernal sensitivity, a halo of clarity that refreshes the heart without blinding the eyes. How delightful it would be to remain here in contemplation and forget all contemporaneousness!

And so now, with regrets, we leave Pisa. Driven by a gesticulating hackney coachman, a nervous horse takes us through deserted stone-paved streets devoid of sidewalks. We pass by the prison; under the blazing sun, a young man kneeling in the pose of Giotto's *San Francesco* is praying for his incarcerated father; a tawny-blond girl of amber complexion with the profile of a Gozzoli[2] is screaming and running after us; her eyes are violet, her naked feet are beautiful. In the piazza of the seminary are very old plane trees; at the opposite ends of a stone bench a man and a woman are seated right where we saw them five hours earlier. We pass by the palazzo where Byron lived nearby the Shelleys—one imagines the visits of Byron to Shelley's sister, their colloquies at night in the Camposanto, and the long walks they took along the lively wide quays. Further on is the custom's office, and finally the railroad station, where our dank, smoky black train is pulling in.

---

[2] Benozzo Gozzoli (1420–1497) was an Italian Renaissance painter from Florence. A pupil of Fra Angelico, Gozzoli is best known for a series of murals in the Magi Chapel of the Palazzo Medici-Riccardi, depicting festive, vibrant processions with fine attention to detail and a pronounced international Gothic influence.

⊕

Now on to Florence: Firenze. Coming from Pisa, Firenze is first seen sporadically through the colonnades of her white birch trees bordering the roads. Firenze appears arrayed in yellow and old rose, stretched out in the basin of her amphitheaters, her domes scintillating like the mysterious mixture of an alchemic spirit simmering in a vast crucible. From its iridescent surface, delicately-hued light vapors are rising, and her edifices are the brilliant crests that will a little later shine as pure, splendid precious stones!

Piazza della Signoria! Scene of so many riots, so many passions, strifes and struggles, hatreds and yearnings, where so much blood was spilled! It was on this square that Savonarola was hanged and burned on May 23, 1498; it was here that Michelangelo and Bandinelli confronted each other. We followed the alley where Cellini found the young pages who served as models for his precious statuettes; a little further on we found the spot where Giotto meditated, and where Fra Angelico prayed; perhaps it was from this very window that Filippo Lippi[3] jumped in his haste to keep a gallant rendezvous.

This particular evening, from the Ponte Vecchio, I can hear a baritone and a tenor singing popular ballads. Their beautiful voices wafting over the slow rippling waters of the peaceful moonlit Arno come back to me again and again from afar, more tenuous, enriched by the echo from the quay opposite, where Venetian-like, the water bathes the arches and pilasters sustaining them.

The old Fiorenza is dead, but she wills to survive. How-

---

[3] Fra Filippo Lippi (c. 1406–1469), Florentine painter in the second generation of Renaissance artists.

ever, her life is not spontaneous anymore; the barbarous tribes from the North galvanize her; her intellect has been reduced to searching piously among her venerable archives; her sensitivity merely serves to copy the magnificence of her honored, centuries-old glories.

In any case, the faces of its women are somewhat non-descript, although their bodies retain elegance; the men, whether shaven or bearded, still recall Renaissance profiles; one sees officers whose mien enhances their sober uniforms; we note some attractive adolescents, and men whose faces are staid or cruel.

As a whole, the race has kept its nervous elegance; she still paws or prances as do ponies harnessed to small tilbury carriages; she still labors with the detached mood of the slender-legged horses drawing the Sicilian carts of its peasantry.

The Uffizi Galleries and the Palazzo Vecchio—what serene majesty exudes from the former, what austere majesty from the latter! On a public square stand a dozen chefs-d'oeuvre helter-skelter, making our Parisian squares seem poor in comparison!

The bust of Lorenzo di Medici depicts a massive, powerful, common face; the jaws of an athlete, irregular eyebrows, the nose of a brave man—the vigorous draft anticipating the finely-chiseled features of his sons.

The portraits of the Venetian school, solidly structured, sketched without lineaments, in deep warm, vibrant colors—as expressed by Balzac in *The Unknown Masterpiece* (the portrait of a captain by an unknown artist).

The Virgin of Botticelli offering her inexpressible face within a round frame.

The admirable Adoration of the Magi, an unfinished

work of Leonardo's, in the mysterious chiaroscuro from which admirable sphinx-like figures stand out.

See the works of Filippo Lippi, of Lorenzo di Credi: masters of the suave, masters of harmony, who alone have known how to conciliate minutiae of detail with synthesis of the whole. Notice the fluidic, gemlike, aerial color, proof of great craftsmanship without affectation!

They lived in want, in dirt, in poverty, in dreams. Filippo Lippi had six daughters.

The little streets on the right between the Borsa (stock exchange) and Santa Croce still have many houses dating from the time of Dante Alighieri. The center of the city used to be the old Roman Fiorenza.

The ghetto is between the Palazzo Strozzi and the Victor Emmanuel Square. The Cascines—a modern park.[4]

We attended Mass at the Piazza Duomo (Santa Maria del Fiore); a Mass worthy of lords, celebrated with decorum by prelates who have chiseled profiles and elegant, graceful hands—a Mass celebrated in a bare basilica, where are neither benches nor chairs, no collection taken, and very few faithful, yet a place of worship filled with masterpieces; a cathedral whose singers wear costumes, whose sanctuary as large as a stage is peopled with red capes and purple mantelletas. The archbishop is wearing an old-rose chasuble; he performs the usual complicated rites, he multiplies blessings and gestures; the assisting clergy kisses his hand at

[4] Situated on the right bank of the River Arno, the Parco delle Cascine (Castine Park) is the largest public park of Florence. In addition to the river Arno, it is bordered by the river Mugnone and the canal Macinante, built in 1563. Originally serving as a hunting reserve and to raise cattle, the Cascine was a vast farm belonging to Alessandro and Cosimo I de Medici.

appropriate intervals. He knows how to genuflect gracefully; he elegantly elevates the chalice to his lips; and the thurifers produce thick clouds of incense.

Seen from our balcony of the Lungarno Acciainoli, the sunsets have a unique beauty—the same limpid hues one finds even in the black pigments of the canvasses of Piero Perugino, da Vinci, and Botticelli. The clouds reflected upon the Arno color the water greenish-yellow and lavender-blue. The picturesque constructions of the Ponte Vecchio is a symphony of all shades of chestnut-brown, rose, and gray; meanwhile the medieval bells from the campaniles intermingle their antique timbres. A small craft is plying upstream, leaving a grayish-green wake out of which Botticelli would have made a Virgin's mantle; and the voice of a singer reverberating by the stone quays accentuates the nostalgic solitude of twilight.

As regards its body, the beauty of this ancient city still remains, but the angel who brought it forth five centuries ago has departed; and we, its faithful, must make the effort of a searchingly pious evocation in order to find within its secret atmosphere the still quivering wake of its magnificent wings.

We passed rapidly through the Bargello (Palazzo del Podesta) this morning. This massive, severe construction, the vaults of which, from the 13th to the 15th centuries, resounded with the cries of the populace, and from the 16th century on from the screams of unfortunate prisoners subjected to torture and the rack, today experiences nothing but the silent chanting of its perfect statues.

The Adonis, the Drunken Bacchus, the Brutus, the Victory, the Holy Family, the David, the Leda, are seven examples of Michelangelo's genius. The Bacchus is both a sensual and a serene epic: his fat belly, curved legs, rounded broad shoulders, and face are strophes of silent voluptuousness.

The beauty of the Holy Family is profound. It is not mystical: it represents human splendor, Platonic heroism, extended to womanhood. Human also are the graceful urchins of Donatello.

Cellini is already too wise.

The Tabernacle of the Orcagna found in one of the corners of Church of Orsanmichele is a gigantic jewel.

As to the Lippis, Benozzo Gozzolis, Angelicos, they encircled their faces; so is the portrait of Albrecht Dürer's father, where the eyebrows are painted one by one, such as is found in the enlarged illuminated mediaeval manuscripts. Yet all these masterpieces, these oeuvres-d'art, are initiators in the true sense of the word, because from them all Italy proceeds. In the old cloister of San Marco, when you look at the pale frescos that the angelic brother has placed in each cell by the window, your heart will throb if a taste for heaven is within you; you will imbibe these graces, fervors, and ecstasies as you would a deliciously strong wine; and you will be overcome by monastic purity. A statue depicting a person rapt in prayer sets in motion those attitudes Botticelli favored; the particular anatomy of a crucified man recalls a Donatello; the certain shape of a taut eyelid is found again in the Leonardos; the particular fold of a mantle is recognizable among the Gozzolis, Lippis, and all the others. But not one of them is as absorbed by the spirit of love as this naive Dominican who sobs for the love of Jesus before daring to portray him.

Fra Benedetto, spiritual brother of the Angelico, shows the same piety and the same color sense in the magnificent illuminations of his antiphonals. In order to understand their art, to follow it through from its incipience to the point whence it issues still cloaked in the sanctuaries of the soul, long hours of reverie and contemplation on the hills of Fiesole are necessary. Because, everything in man, as well as in the universe, comes down from its eternal pedestal in three successive steps, as if the proportion between the diameters of all spheres to their organic circumferences were the immutable formula of a divine geometry.

Back of any work stands the science that organized its mental and material scaffolding; but, prior to this discursive science, the intuitive conception took place by means of which the visiting angel made himself known to his host the artist; while far beyond the worlds, beyond man and forms, in the gracious stillness of his perenniality, shines this handsome, resplendent angel.

If it be the everlasting Italy that you want to study, commence with its initiators: Dante, Giotto, Michelangelo. Everything proceeds from these three, as extensions and developments of one or several of their qualities.

As to the mysterious Leonardo, he is a blossom without roots. Born outside of the law from the very beginning, he remains an exception in every way. If the others give us a taste of the most delightful berries from the tree of life, he offers us those from the tree of science—which he likely sought during his youthful adventures on the borders of the Nile. Grandson of the red Etruscans, his atavistic instinct permitted him to find once again the spiritual sons of the Atlantean sages at the pyramids; and if he did not want to discipline himself sufficiently to win the crown of an adept, his intelligence was nonetheless vast enough to encompass and probe certain mysteries, and his soul fervent enough to divulge them to the world under an aesthetic form. In any case, another disciple of unknown masters, the enigmatic Rosenkreutz was preparing at the same time to reveal a more social aspect of these antediluvian arcana.

Hence, if you want to understand Leonardo, take up Plato again as harbinger. Then forget him. Later, try to be accepted and received among the lesser-known Brahmans, known as those "with knowledge." Try to be accepted by and received in the home of some venerable, scraggly white-bearded Southeast Asian. At the feet of the naked ascetic seated under a banyan tree, your legs crossed on a rug of Kouta, or reclining on an ebony couch in the midst of aromatic opium smoke, listen from the bottom of your poor, famished, naked heart to the age-old maxims of esoteric wisdom.

After months of such abstraction, then, perhaps, you will be able to feel that mysterious, unstable, vibrating point—unique and infinite, not yet matter, not quite essence anymore—which the sages of Israel represented under the sixth character of the Hebraic alphabet, the number six being for them that of harmonious and central beauty. You will find this beam of Libra's zodiacal scale described by the Hindu Ananda, represented by the Hermetic androgyne, depicted by the Chinese dragon above the rice field. Theoretically, you will know the inexpressible stasis of the authentic Rosicrucians, and maybe their Elijah spirit will accept you as courser.

Know that all this is to be found in the chiaroscuro of Leonardo, in the smile of his Gioconda; it is in the ambiguous breast of the Precursor; also in the folds of the eyelids he sketches; it is in the contour of his Virgins' hands.

But take care! for at that moment Lucifer and Jesus might be mistaken for twins.

If Leonardo is the magus in the realm of painting, the Angelico is its saint. The former represents audacity, intelligence, is a demigod; the latter is humility, innocence, love. Our culture and our modern era are closer to Leonardo; that is why we will admire the little Fra Angelico longer.

And so on we went, climbing the ascending road that winds around the lovely haughty hill. Just as we left the newly-built suburbs of Florence, we found ourselves in the elegant countryside with yellow and rose-colored houses strewn here and there; homes nesting amid green bamboos or grayish-green olive trees, tall somber pines or larch, a realm with walls and embankments where grapes multiply upon the lattices of shady pergolas; where two tall noble cypresses indicate the entrance of villas, and the double-file outline the terraced orchards is a pleasure to the eyes.

Here we find the domain of Dante. Only the earth and the rocks are the same as those that bear the invisible imprints of the old poet's footsteps, for all the edifices were rebuilt by the Portinari family in the fifteenth century.

Along one of the side paths we came to the venerable, noble, dignified eleventh-century church of the Badia that Brunelleschi built for Pico della Mirandola and the Platonic Academy. On the other side of the new road one finds the convent of the "Hounds of The Lord" (*Domini Canes*), where, after coming down from his natal hills, Fra Angelico received in the penumbra of his contemplations the seed of light that would someday grow into San Marco. O! peaceful abodes amid our contemporary carnage, chaste islets scattered in the swamps of frightful corruptions, fertile seeds of love and humility set amid the weeds of desultory erudition, dialecticism, and intellectual dilettantism— you are today desolate, forsaken, parched, thanks to the indifference of the people among whom God has placed you. Woe to these people! We see them today stricken with powerlessness, incapable of creating; virtuosi yes, but not artists; critics yes, but not discoverers; sensitive yes, but not with a sense of the divine; lovers yes, but infamous vice spreads in the dark alleys as well as on the resplendent thoroughfares; yes, some inhabit palaces, but they are devoid of will and personality, while others lodge in hovels, but with anger and envy in their heart.

The Academy of Fine Arts (Galleria dell'Accademia di Firenze) remains as the revelation of Michelangelo. This man, into whose intimacy Romain Rolland's biography introduces us, had never known anything but the sorrow of living. Everything was against him, everyone betrayed him; in the paganish Italy of his day everything chilled his heart. With titanic vigor he dedicated himself to fulfilling the thought of Dante, but from these descriptive scenes the only one he experienced on earth was hell; hence the personages he depicts are all superhuman in vigor and strength, in breadth of soul, in combative energy, in addition to the overwhelming powers that possess them.

His rough drafts are his most touching works. Not a single sculptor from that time on has been able to incarnate such vibrant reality in stone. Compared to him, Rodin is but a pupil. All that hunger for love, all that fulgurant passion for the divine, all that powerless dolor, all that exhausted paroxysm of effort that his marble statues possess in such gigantic measure, exudes from them, giving them living, palpitating contours; and the air in which they bathe vibrates as from a flamboyant halo. Even a blind man touching these Slaves that he carved could sense their palpitating anguish.

In fact, in any rough draft is to be found a part, a perceptible presence, of the artist: the music of the secret colloquy between him and his genius still floats about, though inaudible to physical ears. But, provided we know how to love, our heart hears that presence. The soul of this likely Prometheus throbs forever within these rough-hewn marbles.

Also, in an unfinished work of art, one can follow all the sculptor's probings, all the chisel's cuts, his spontaneous spurs of imagination, his endeavors and hesitancies, accompanying the secrets of his craft. Craftsmanship is the task at hand, that which one can learn; but what no school can offer is the artist's struggle with the angel. Or rather, let us admit that we do not have to struggle with the angels heaven sends us, for the combat their arrival occasions is with what is obscure, obfuscated, unintelligent, base, ignorant, and slothful within us—with what resists the spirit, trembles at the prevision of sufferings, and would prefer slumber on the soft cushion of "What is the use?" There again, to master one's self is of primordial importance.

Howsoever that may be, Michelangelo's face bears the stigmas of these struggles. Such lofty brows always denote the faculty of divination into the Mysteries; the nose, which must have been salient during his youth, indicates great sentimentality; its wide root denotes well-developed faculties of perception and objectivity, just as the outward bulging orbital arch denotes the gift of form, of grouping, and of construction. The hollow temple reveals that he was taciturn, the long ears imply he was wise and very ancient; the cranial height denotes morality, a thirst for what is beautiful and real, a religious bent, and uncompromising convictions. His furrowed brow and gaunt, sunken cheeks reveal his meditative nature, his griefs and sorrows; while his muscular hands give proof of the untiring energy exerted in his work.

Saint-Laurent is a noble basilica filled with noble works of art, where Brunelleschi and Donatello hold sway. But one finds two very sorry items as well therein. In a nook by the side of a well stands a charming marble basin, but the bottom is filled with rubbish; and in one of the transept chapels are four hideous colored-plaster figures holding candelabras of such poor taste that even our tradesmen on the rue St Sulpice would be ashamed to sell them.

The adjoining cloister is noble too. The ancient sacristy is a marvel of pride and wealth; but the chapel of St Ignatius at Loyola is still more sumptuous. As to the new sacristy, it is the worthy jewel-case for the masterpieces it shelters. The circles and squares of black marble decorating its walls, the proportions of the heights, widths, and diameters, the dimensions of its two sepulchers, conjointly form a harmonious whole. Yet were it permissible to make a choice where a colossal being such as Michelangelo is concerned, I would choose his august Virgin rather than his sepulchral monuments. In her we discover more of the man than the Casa Buonarroti has given us—that artist who started merely as a good, honest man, who became a great citizen, and who finally ended his glorious life in wisdom and sanctity.

⊕

To our right we see Bellagio, where for nine years Arnold Boecklin conceived his Romantic Art form.[5] A little higher up, a magnificent ramp bordered with cypresses leads to the wrought-iron gates of the Villa Medici, where Lorenzo il

---

[5] Arnold Boecklin (1827–1901), Swiss symbolist painter from Basel.

Magnifico used to relax reading the pleasant verses of Politian. There, both he and his brother Guliano would come to mourn the beautiful Simonetta, whose life had been nipped in the bud of youth; there too he would poetize for Lucrezia Donati; there also he discoursed with Pico della Mirandola, who came from Badia at twilight to read to him his "Commentary upon Genesis"; there he would laugh with the kind bourgeois clerks and laymen, the responsible citizens who own some sunny piece of land and hold office. He would banter and exchange pleasantries with the peasants whose songs he collected, savoring the scandalous or tragic tales as much as he relished the vituperations of the apocalyptic Girolama Savonarola.

So, as one ascends from one terrace to another along ancient broken-stone paths to olive groves partitioned by walls of cypresses, one reaches the princely villas whose walls are decorated with potted plants, their pilasters adorned with the Florentine lion and its symbolic dog.

As we came the end of the rear wall of the Villa Medici, we turned around and saw the sheer splendor of a Dantesque décor. It is nothing, and yet seems to be the ascent to Paradise—a wide low-step stairway on the right of which are the ancient retaining walls of a garden. On its left one sees a peaceful countryside and two rows of cypresses, several centuries old, impassible, unique; and between them the ascending ramp follows a slow winding curve that finally ends at a triple-arch vaulted loggia. Out of a small door a tall white-clad monk is emerging.

⊕

Now to the city of Fiesole. Its great square is immense, giving the impression of a large empty frame, yet for the past three hundred years men have been living on this spot. The mysterious Etruscans cultivated its soil, built enormous, thick defensive walls. They propagated the bearded, muscled athletic type with the slender, delicately jointed limbs and glib tongue still found among the peasantry. Then the Romans, with a force that centuries could only modify, left their imprint upon the language, architecture, and customs. Their genius refined the Etruscan minds, rendered their bodies more supple, quickened their gestures, and chiseled their features. It gave them ambition, taste, vitality, impetus.

As we proceeded, we noticed how massive granitic rockbeds and slate strata projecting out amid the plant life support walls and houses, and nourish the magnificently formed trees; also, how man's industrious ingenuity crowns this dual effort by erecting noble monuments and palaces, by filling the large Signa vases with luxurious plants, by nestling lovely statuettes in the hollows of the walls, by multiplying porticos, colonnades, and bas-reliefs.

Above this vast square, Santa Maria Primanera retains, in spite of unhappy restorations, some vestiges of its austere tenth-century medieval designs. Alongside, the old thirteen-century city hall induces you to visit its scant archaeological collections; but if the beggars, the straw-basket hawkers, and the carters give you some respite, forget about the seminary and enter directly into the simple and imposing nave of the Cathedral. The three lateral aisles, the noble vaulted arches, the terraced choir, and the somber crypt will enable you to evoke the antique period from the eleventh to the fifteenth century, when the faithful en masse believed, felt, became involved in, and were transfigured under the hidden influence of the Holy Spirit through whom these stones had been assembled.

Today, the seminary is half empty, the bishop's palace rooms are no longer buzzing with the activities of zealous secretaries; and the Franciscan convent built later on the site where the Capitol of the Roman Faesula (Fiesole) formerly stood, regrets its congregation of monks. People of small means now live lives of penury amid flies in hovels along the ill-smelling alleyways.

As regards monks and priests, it is interesting to study the clergy and friars in Italy. First of all, they wear beautiful habits. The priests do not wear the tight cassocks or narrow quilted overcoats worn in France; their robes are ample; most of them wear a sleeveless coat (usually held by a simple cord at the neck) falling in sculptured folds in back.

Both monks and secular priests have remarkable faces, in which one may read more passion, finesse, and even vice, than fervor and virtue. Never are they insignificant; they look boldly around; some do not neglect trying to impress the beautiful young tourists. They live enjoying their surroundings, the gentle breezes, the fragrant herbs, the shapely trees, the horizons, while exchanging pleasantries with the humble people. The Capucine friars often carry extraordinary umbrellas, and as one gets too close to them, one senses that they most surely must be enemies of sanitary ablutions.

In this highly-strung landscape, the sunsets have the same moving, passionate grace as a dying young woman who knows too little about love. We would often go down to contemplate these settings from the St Jerome Loggia, or take the path ascending sharply to the portal of St Francis, or go north to the Forte Belvedere.

The perfumes wafting up from the valley would interblend like a symphony; the fragrance from the old olive groves, cypresses, and cork-oak woods, warmed all the day long under the ardent rays of the sun, would finally distill this natural alchemy in the fresh breezes descending from the bluish Apennines at twilight. Above this fragrant tonic would play the peppery smells of carnations, the sweet aroma of irises and lilies, the pathos of the innumerable anonymous herbs piercing the walls, disjoining the old cobblestones, nestling at the base of trees, and finally encroaching upon yards and terraces.

To the east, mauve vapors deepen into violet, then change into gray tints; the elongated clouds are now suspended immobile, like white sailing ships upon a tranquil sea in the darkening blue sky.

An ashy vapor rises from the plain where Florence dreams in an elegant pose. She is the center of the picture. All the graduated shades of greens, blues, yellows, and grays of the surroundings converge toward her rosy form. Above her, the smoky azure of the east slowly veers into the old-rose hues that gradually ripen into the triumphant vivid red of the Apollonian sphere hovering over a delicate balustrade of lyrical haze to our right. The sun sinks jerkily, as if it were descending the steps of an invisible stairway. Soon it has become nothing but an arc, which now disappears, leaving as witnesses of its invisible presence, horizontally, in the crimson, and with an amethyst and topaz vault in the firmament. To our left, meanwhile, its pale sister moon sheds its eerie light amidst the twinkling lights of the stars.

This dramatic elegy, with its unfathomable wealth of splendorous effects, is reenacted each evening by nature. At that very moment, as well as at dawn, something happens in the secondary atmosphere that is perceptible only to those whose eyes are open. The founders of Brahmanism and of Catholicism were well aware of it, as they instituted their prayers at both twilights: dawn and sunset. At these moments, as well as at noon and midnight, the reciprocal positions of the earth and sun signify the four changes occurring in the polarization of universal magnetism. These are nodes within the vibrations of the black light, which man may profit from by making use of this wide-open door to penetrate into the invisible. If he belongs to a religious collectivity, an elemental spirit awaits to guide him, and may even accompany him back after presenting him a fruit from the marvelous garden. If the devout man is alone, he makes his incursion at his own risk.

However, only the monks in Catholicism and the Brahmans of India get up at midnight to accomplish the fourth (or the first) of these salutations, because the petitions the Indian recites are a sort of *Ave Maria*: they too, at these moments of rest, worship the eternal Virgin, the very pure Mother of God.

⊕

The cemetery of Fiesole is one of the most moving places we encountered. It stretches along the northern flank of the San Francesco hill by a path that used to be called Capitol Street at the time of the sons of Romulus. One ascends to it via an alley bordered with solemn ancient cypresses, the silent sentinels who render funereal honor to the dead. This is the path where at night would pass the black-hooded penitents with their cowls and torches bringing the men back to their welcoming mothers.

Beneath the arcades of the Camposanto are the sepulchers of the rich. The graves of the poor are in the earth with a mere cross marker and clump of flowering plants. At the foot of most of these tombs burns a candle piously maintained by the family. We see children pulling weeds nearby. A prostrate figure—a poor peasant woman is reciting the rosary aloud as she kisses the photograph of her lost child, while the little one who replaced the elder plays in the sand close by.

We keep climbing; bordered as usual with vigilant cypresses, the upper embankments uphold very ancient olive trees with twisted trunks through whose branches climb grapevines. Still further up, to the left, we discover three levels of adjoining hills shading off from gray-green to lilac tones; before us, far below lie the Etrusco-Roman ruins of a circus. To our right, spread over the flank of this mystical hill, pinkish from the rays of the setting sun, the houses of Fiesole stand out as a troupe of youngsters tired out from exertions in the sun.

The bells are now tolling for a belated office; first one rings, then another, then all together—the campanile of the Episcopal Duomo, those of San Francesco, those from San Alessandro, even the far-off ones from the Badia and San Dominico—this ensemble sings, moans, gongs, intermingles with undulations that slowly rise, descend, and hover at the mercy of the atmospheric currents, echoing like an invisible albatross with broad, widespread wings balanced upon the invisible ocean of sound.

Thus the rosy-hued heavenly light increases; magnified progressively from grace to splendor, it stirs the volutes of wings that the east wind elongates; one could compare them to angels sinuously passing by in their long-trailing robes, holding in their uplifted hands some precious fruit from paradise. Ah! The bells of Fiesole, the light of Fiesole, the hieratic cypresses, faithful guardians of the living and the dead; the elegant contours of Tuscan horizons, terrestrial representations of eternal hills, havens of delicate and proud beauty, echoes of cherubinic conversations—how seductive you still are even in your present forsaken state!

Due to your iniquity, all the vulgarity, lewdness, arrogance, and avariciousness of men settled little by little in the bottom of the crucible of centuries. Your foreign tyrants have made you take stock of yourselves, so that out of these fermentations, out of these cupidities, laments, and tears, what was eternal in your aspirations, what was superhuman in your efforts and celestial in your beauty rays through today with a purer light.

All alchemies, my friends, do not originate in laboratories; and fire assumes many more invisible as well as inexpressible forms than those of its physical aspects.

At our hotel yesterday, a banquet of Orphéonists took place. The brass band, the so-called "fanfare" of Fiesole, entertained with the Compiobbi band. Naturally, there were after-dinner speeches and a few songs. We could read deep pleasure upon the various bronzed leathery faces; we noticed how intently they listened, the excellent mimicry and gusto of the orators, how they fascinated and held their audience's attention—all of which offered us an instructive canvas, which, seen from another angle, seemed pitiful.

These good people were Garibaldists. People threw flowers upon them whenever they paraded; many houses were festooned with red garlands, the enthusiastic conviction and hopes of the crowd floated in the air; interminable applause cheered this most developed socialism; and clamors against the king and the pope hardly ever toned down in that large smoke-filled malodorous hall.

After all, for centuries, they believed implicitly in the

Church and in their lords; they had been hoaxed, pressured, burnt, often killed for their present demands to be justified; they now hold and look for other illusions. May it please heaven that their present search be somewhat less painful and less stressful than the one preceding.

The sincerity of the people, of the masses, is admirable. During these evenings I observed how the passersby, grouped upon the Mino di Fiesole terrace, were listening to the Orphéonists' music; and might I add that the skill of these village orchestras caught me by surprise.

In the crowd were some very handsome types of men, most of them attentively listening with the same immobility, fixity, and inner tension that Fra Angelico so well portrayed. One of them was a particularly admirable example. He was a tall peasant, still young, thin and bony, his face matte-complexioned, clean-shaven. In his eyes, in the shape of his hooded eye-lids (situated high within the contour of his temples and maxillaries) there was such finesse—an earnest fervor seldom seen, and extinct today.

The soul of the Poverello of Assisi could not have found or chosen a more expressive or nobler sheath in which to embody itself.

# PART III

Letters

.

## Letter to *L'Echo du Merveilleux*

October 15, 1910

I am but a solitary student. I do not belong to any research association, to any visible esoteric or religious fraternity. The few friends who share my conception regarding esotericism have the good fortune of being unknown, and the wisdom to remain so.

I have delved into many subjects since 1887, when these studies began to interest me passionately. I never had the material means to acquire the books I sought, and time was lacking; but destiny compensated me by placing on my path the authorized representatives of the highest traditions. Propriety has always prevented me from divulging to anyone what those extraordinary but obscure men considered as inviolable secrets.

Rabbis have communicated their secret manuscripts to me; alchemists admitted me to their laboratories. Many a night Sufis, Buddhists, and Taoists, have taken me along to the abode of their gods. A Brahman permitted me to copy his table of mantra, and a Yogi imparted to me the secrets of contemplation. But one evening, after meeting a certain person, all that those admirable men had taught me became as nothing, as attenuated as mist rising at dusk from the overheated earth.

All my small books on esotericism, all my articles in occult journals, all the classes I led at the Hermetic School, were necessarily punctuated with gaps or times of reticence. At best, these arid essays had the merit of drawing the attention of seekers, and of calling forth deeper research and work. As for myself, I along with a few close friends have explored all extant esotericisms with fervent sincerity and the utmost desire for success. But none of these certitudes, once attained, seemed to be The Certitude.

Very early in life I had the chance of discovering and understanding the Illuminati, especially Louis-Claude de Saint-Martin—and, through him, the genial Jacob Boehme, in whose dense work pre-Krishnaite theosophy, German philosophy, and modern philosophy are found in abbreviated form. From there, after having followed the prevalent illusion that prompts us to seek afar treasures that in fact providence places within our reach, I finally came to the mystics. Do we not run after what we think is hidden? We know nothing about our own religion. It does not interest us. And yet its dogma and liturgy are the most complete presentation of integral knowledge existing on earth at this time. All that theologians have so far written is not the twentieth part of the truths contained in its teachings. Everything is there in Catholicism: the science of the mineral as well as the science of the soul; the art of being a head of state or ruler as well as practicing the art of the medical man; the power of the thaumaturgist as well as the tactics of the sociologist. Please know that the opinion I here express is not that of a faithful of the Church of Rome, but that of a direct disciple of the gospel—that same gospel which we are so prone to discard in favor of the Eastern religions that we tend to regard as pseudo-tabernacles of the sole truth.

Such considerations as these explain how I was led to draw attention to Boehme, Johann Georg Gichtel, and William Law, by writing about these mystics—generally unknown in France—yet who in my opinion attained as elevated a state as the most celebrated doctors and saints.

But if Boehme and St John of the Cross have much in

common, Swedenborg and Paracelsus differ, and are as con-
flicting as Catholicism, Babism, Islam, Buddhism, Brahmanism, etc. There is no room for sentimentality when
examining theosophical notions. It is not true that all religions are one. If this were so, their adepts would not murder one another, whether with sword or calumny. The
sentimentality-drenched phrases of the dyed-in-the-wool
exponents of the "unity of all religions" are born from a
flaw in logic. In the Absolute (so they claim) all is one;
therefore (so they claim) forms in the Relative must be one
also. Absolutely not! The Hindu *trimurti* is neither the
Christian *trinity* nor the Pythagorean *ternary*. Jesus and the
Buddha are neither the same principle nor two functions of
the same principle. Gnosis and the gospels do not lead to
the same goal.

One must read in the texts what is there, not what one
would wish to find there. In spiritual experiences, one must
observe what happens, not what some pseudo-master
affirms should happen. Never give up your right to exam-
ine and test. That is why I wrote the books *On Fakirism*,
*The Magic Letters*, and *Occult Medicine*.

Where does this certitude come from, it will be asked,
and by what right this presumption of authority? Today's
intellectuality understands the mystic very poorly; nor do I
claim to be one. To me, that word represents so elevated a
state that I can only hold it as my ideal. Would I, then, be
my own criterion? No, I know only that the Father is all.
And yet man believes the Father to be nothing, or next to
nothing. Why, two thousand years ago, if someone went
out on the roads, capturing souls with a simple glance and
raising them to the threshold of uncreated light—why
couldn't that someone renew, whenever he pleased, these

spiritual cures, according to the encounters he provokes along the mysterious paths of the invisible?

My God is the Absolute, the essence of the Absolute; and as such, He is closer to me than the most beautiful of gods, than the tenderest of spouses. To hear his miraculous voice, it suffices to cease listening to created beings; to feel his all-powerful ineffable kindness, it suffices to stop desiring created beings.

One acclaims Lao-Tze, Moses, Pythagoras, Dionysius the Areopagite, the Rosicrucians. But they are small, flickering flames. They have not seen the billionth part of what there is to see. They have also raised fences and built guard rails between us and the Father! But that should not be. For there is nothing between man and God except the willful perversion of man. To come to see that we know nothing; to experience that we can do nothing; to verify that heaven is here within us and that our Friend constantly enfolds us within his blessed arms—this is the lesson of Jesus. This I have attempted to say by publishing five volumes of lectures on the gospels,[1] along with *The Mystic Breviary, Our Spiritualistic Duty, Mystical Forces*, and *Initiations*.

**Letter to the *Fraterniste***
March 10, 1913
In the most recent issue of your esteemed newspaper, someone showed me a letter in which M. Felix Guinot mentions (in far too flattering terms) the ideas to the propagation of which I have dedicated myself, as well as the note with which you concluded this remarkable missive.

---

[1] *The Childhood of Jesus, The Sermon on the Mount, The Healings of Christ, The Kingdom of God,* and *The Crowning of His Work*.

In response to this note, please let me tell you that the Catholicism I recommend the study of is *not* clericalism. It is the theology of such men as St Augustine, Duns Scotus, and the Thomists. It is the liturgy of such men as St Ambrose and St Benedict. It is the religion of a St Francis of Assisi, a St Vincent de Paul, a Cure d'Ars (St John-Marie Vianney). These great men and their great works seem to me more worthy of our admiration than Oriental syntheses (no matter how profound they may be), and than the superhuman adepts who built them. I never meant to recommend parochial theologies, intrigues between various religious orders, or the innumerable devotions that keep decadent paganism alive in our times. In short, I keep close to the gospel, and give credence to its commentators only if by their actions they have proven the sincerity of their faith.

What is more, when I propose Catholicism to seekers in this way, I am addressing only those (so numerous today) who need theories, systems, and rituals; those who still believe in and hold solely to intelligence, who do not feel the immediate presence of the Friend in their hearts, and who imagine God as a far-distant being.

And so you see, Monsieur, I am not a Catholic or a rationalist, an occultist or a spiritualist. I am merely trying to call attention to the eternal voice that speaks in the depth of the heart of each one of us. This voice is Jesus.

And though Jesus seems so outdated to us modern men, I think we have not yet understood the thousandth part of the teachings contained in the gospels. How should we let him teach us?—that is our sole problem. All the rest (as our delightful Verlaine said) is but literature.

**Letter regarding** *Les Amitiés Spirituelles* (Friends in Spirit)
Our association exists only for those who do not feel the
need of an exteriorized form of religion. Those for whom
visible or exterior rites are necessary must obey their spiritual needs. When one wants to profit from the help of a
religious organization, it is essential that they be immersed
in it totally. Hence, such people are not benefited by
remaining with the Friends in Spirit. On the other hand,
one cannot (without being a hypocrite) claim to be a Catholic without actually being one—and the same applies to
any other denomination. Our spirit cannot follow two
paths at the same time.

As for us, we don't look for a qualified endorsement.
Such sympathy is ineffective, both for those who give it and
for those who are the objects of it. Our Friends in Spirit
association is not a church. It is not against any group or
society whatsoever. It is established for Christ. Our sole aim
is to help people see and know that Christ is the sole Son of
God, and that our only requisite is to exercise charity
(love)—which is his only commandment.

As to following the rites of the religion in which we were
born, we say that it is a just and fair attitude. Jesus observed
the rites of Judaism. To the parents who ask us, we always
recommend that their children be baptized, make their first
communion, go through a religious ceremony for marriage,
and also for burial. In our estimation, we have no cause
to concern ourselves with possible defects in the Church's
teachings, or with the dignity or the indignity of certain
priests or clergymen. We do not stand in judgment of our
brothers.

When we say that Catholicism is the most complete
among the Christian religions, we do not mean to say one

has to become a Catholic. We merely express our personal opinion, that is all. We should not change our religion save when, in all conscience, we cannot remain in the one we were born into. We do not wish to lead souls toward or turn them away from any church, because we believe that religion in spirit and in truth is essentially practicing the tenets of the gospel.

May those who feel the need of the Church and its rites be benefited. As for those who tend towards unmediated communion with God, they can abstain from ecclesiastical ceremonies, provided that, in spite of the deprivation of this aid, they are committed to the realization of the gospel with the same constancy as the practicing faithful.

# Letters to Friends

April 1913
Let me call your attention to practical, material, effort. Do not let a good thought or an enthusiastic feeling pass without a positive sanction. This act, seemingly sterile at first, is most profitable: its fruits ripen fast, miracles occur, prayers become ardent, feelings of despondency and disappointment are transmuted into joy. In the core of your heart you have the certitude that Christ is at your side, that he sees, hears, and supports you. Cultivate the bracing feeling of this ineffable presence. Stand by as "nothingness" before this resplendent plenitude. Always ask yourself: what would my Master do in the circumstances in which I find myself? Thus it is that one begins to love everything: life, love, even sorrow and pain. Evil seems then to be nothing but weakness begging for our help, and men nothing but victims of the Adversary. To benefit from these communions, we have to become attentive and obedient to the lessons we receive from our Master, and from events—because heaven expects more from us than merely experiencing personal joy.

April 1913
I can assure you of an ever-growing union among us. The dreams of several among you corroborate this assertion. The luxurious surroundings and atmosphere of some of these dreams, in contradistinction to the relatively simple fare of the meals, prove that we are still too concerned about various gods, no matter what we may think. I beg of you, let us remain simple, let us think of no one but Christ. In other dreams, where meals are delicious, remember it is

your spirit that is being revivified. Therefore, expect material tribulations.

May 1913

I ask that you consider your work as a very serious endeavor. A few among you prefer individualistic and silent effort. As for me, the Friends in Spirit association exists, it is a living being. The Father has never created any unnecessary being. Hence we must keep alive the genie of true associations (i.e., those associations whose principle is based in heaven), on condition that this unity be in Christ—this being the sole and indispensable condition.

August 1913

A substantive and material discipline helps towards one's moral discipline. For our Association's sake, it is preferable to be too scrupulous rather than too negligent. Each must adapt his total obedience according to the needs of the circumstances. Each of you must reflect on these problems and grow accustomed to resolving them personally within the dignity of your connection with heaven. Discipline is essentially for yourself alone, for your interior and personal life. Your duty—and never forget it—is action, i.e., influencing your environs.

We who remain in the world, who do not take shelter as monks do, must be that much more vigilant and take heed of our conscience, yet all the while keeping it veiled on account of sympathy and grace. As soon as angels hear a command from heaven, that command is executed; nonetheless, owing to their love, even their most repellent missions are transformed into joy. Let us do the same. Let us not forget love.

August 1913

I hope from the bottom of my heart that our Association

will become your concern, that it will be your Association, that each of you considers it as yours, as dependent upon you. Everyone around us has to struggle and fight. We must not only not lag behind, but must keep abreast in the first line of all skirmishes.

My friends, remember me from time to time when you speak to the Father; let us maintain the unity that binds us to Him who brought us together.

October 1913

Let us beware of overt acts of humility. Humility is the most difficult state in the world. All too often our actions are but prevarications of that condition. Have you not heard many a spiritualist say: "I, my dear, I am nothing"? Beware of spiritual pride. Therefore, do not perform systematic or artificial acts of humility, for such are false. Rather, perform acts imbued with real feelings of humility, which no one can observe.

October 1913

It is not the quantitative sum of your prayers that is answered, but their qualitative sum. For example, twenty individuals, each worth four points in sanctity, do not deploy all together a force of eighty, but a force of four. If the solace needed demands a force of a hundred, they will obtain nothing. It is essential that the collective average of their individual sanctity be a hundred. Thus, if I attempt to synchronize your labors, it is not so that these labors yield better results, but so that you might be more firmly knit together. Please believe that I love you all from the depths of my heart.

November 1913

Our group is not opposed to any religion, since it is not a religion. It is an upward movement reviving primitive

Christianity in parallel with the Christianity of the present time. We are not trying to replace the cloisters or the monks, but to fulfill their functions to a greater extent through our practical contact with daily life—from which we do not shy, but on the contrary seek to plunge more deeply into.

If we look at nature, we see that beings develop, not by an increase in volume "on the spot," but by reproduction and radiation afar. The greater the membership of an association, the more difficult to it is conserve the integrity of its spirit. Take for example the Church of Rome, Protestantism, the Jesuits, and Freemasonry. Look at the secret societies of the Far East. These are but temporary organizations born for a certain goal, and dissolve as soon as that goal is attained. They are all bound to their main groups, which in turn are directed by the twelve Unknowns who secretly rule all of Asia. Now look at Christ. He does not centralize the twelve or the seventy; he sends them forth "over the earth."

December 1913

Our mission is to help establish worship in spirit and truth. Beyond that, we have no reason for being. Think about that. I beg of you: get moving. Exert yourselves; burn with an ardent flame, but a steady flame. You must give yourself body and soul to this silent battle; you must fight every minute; you must. I am with you day and night, every day. Thus we remain securely in the luminous shadow of the Friend.

New Year 1914

On this day I ask that inwardly you renew your adherence to a closer union with our eternal Master in order to absorb as much as possible from this living force of realization inherent within Christianity, this force proceeding from the fire of love and sacrifice.

You know it is a living force, because it applies to all projects and situations, to all theoretical, practical, internal as well as external fields of activity; and also, because of its very nature, it brings these innumerable modes back to the eternal unity of the Word.

I expect from you perfection—a concern for perfection in your relationships with all living creatures. Do not dogmatize unless it be asked of you; but neither compromise with what seems to you to be false. Regarding error, do not become party to or fall into any complicities of false tolerance. Point out the path to the straying sheep, but do not force them to take it. Neither let them believe they are on the right path.

Increase your ardor, have more heart: then you will influence and enlighten a great many more people.

Beware of indulging in forbearing patience upon hearing sentimental confessions and turbid thoughts. Listen only to sound and real sufferings in family matters and discords; and in social matters also, particularly those of religious import. Make use of all your ingenuity to alleviate these.

The deeper one grows inwardly, the greater one's influence increases. Be earnest, but neither stiff nor formal. Retain that solemn attitude of serenity and nobility wherein the soul unfurls its wings to lift off, fly, and soar!

Those who come to you feel doubly helped. They have faith in you, first, because they share their conscious, exterior and avowed concerns with you; and second, because of a certain attraction that is both unconscious and entirely spiritual. Take care of satisfying their spiritual needs first; you will then satisfy the former ones better. Be kind to them, charm them from a soul standpoint; be moderate in gestures and words.

But you will not attain perfection in this attitude unless Jesus holds your hand. Extend it toward him, extend it with your whole being, your enthusiasms, forces, aspirations. Also, extend your other hand to the mystical death. Thus will you know life. Thus you will find repose amid the maelstrom of worries, and calm in the pincers of adversity.

Do not ape the lukewarm, who prudently feel out the sand beneath their feet on the shores of the infinite ocean. Throw yourselves into the sea: it will be your most strident call for help. The weak according to the spirit tense up to focus their forces. All of you—yes, you—are strong enough to fathom your weakness. Alternate action with prayer. When you find yourself agonizing, I ask all of you to do more than you ever did before. It matters not whether one dies ten years too soon. When that time comes, what will matter is to have lived fully in God.

February 1914

To follow a good line of conduct, we do not need a long list of precepts, but only a few—that is, on condition that we perpetually put them into practice. For example, this one: Jesus sees us and watches over us: that alone should suffice to make the right decision.

Outward humility is not to be disdained, but it is preferable to adhere to the humility of the heart. It may be that you have to show severity and give commands. If so, let these be mere gestures. One has to conduct oneself according to one's position. Let us cling closer to our Master, watching him vigilantly. Let us not fear taking pains, accepting and bearing the evil that wounds only us. But we must fight against the evil that attacks others.

Receive my fraternal accolade as testimony of the frank and spontaneous affection that is the very atmosphere in which the servants of Jesus breathe.

April 1914

We must be tolerant, not eclectic—which means: we must understand that a man enters the school he is meant to enter; and that any school proceeds to the goal determined by the leaders of that school. Hence, there is no need to be concerned with any evaluations others may make regarding our conduct. Also, there is no need to modify our conduct, except after a thorough examination of comparison with a proper ideal. Let us not worry about what may be said about us— whether they take us to be Jesuits wearing short habits or Franciscan tertiaries or sectarians or braggadocios. Regardless whether this comes from close friends (even the oldest ones) or perhaps from well-regarded people of good character and scientific achievement, it is preferable to keep silent. We must maintain silence at all cost, or at least adopt a non-confrontative attitude.

There is no alternative: either we are just what Christ wants us to be, in which case anything disagreeable that happens must leave us indifferent; or else we do not conform to the desire of Christ, in which case he will know how to set us aright.

What is paramount is that we avoid developing another cult by erecting a little chapel of our own. We must not claim to resuscitate the primitive church, or to serve as model to the metaphysical schools. When faced with any circumstances life deals us, our sole concern should be to realize what in good conscience we judge God's will to be.

Our open-hearted attitude, our simplicity, our dealings with the public, must not permit us to neglect prudence.

We must not use any pressure to bring new recruits into our association; we must not turn any of our interlocutors away from a path in which they feel at home, or still prefer to follow after hearing our explanations.

It is important to shun collective selfishness (which is as terrible as personal selfishness), for it is the great vice of religious associations. It is due to collective selfishness that we have observed the work of an admirable founder, angelic at its inception, become perverted a few years after his death, right down to professing principles and performing acts diametrically contrary to those for the sake of which the order he founded had originally been structured. Whether heaven wants us—The Friends in Spirit—to last only a few years, or to last a few centuries, is not our concern; we must act as if we were to last an eternity.

May 1914

The most frequent occasions of manifesting intolerance occur in our relationships with family, and in our contacts at the office or other place of work. We each have grounds for believing ourselves to be more perspicacious or better informed than our subordinates, our equals, or our superiors—be they wives, husbands, brothers, employees, or bosses. We want to avail ourselves of proving our opinions to be the best, even in insignificant things such as how to draw a line, or where a glass should be placed in a sideboard or cabinet.

For this instinctive tyranny there is but one remedy, which must be heroic and radical, precisely because we are so radically convinced that our views are the right ones. What this means is: never argue, but instead keep quiet; conform to the opinion of others even when we believe our opinion to be right. Among innumerable unimportant acts, we find many occasions of making life unbearable for our family or acquaintances. Let us chop evil out at its roots.

Let us not concern ourselves with who is wrong. Let us accept being somewhat tyrannized rather than ourselves being tyrants. If our friend really is in the wrong, the prayer we address to God at the moment of our voluntary humiliation will show our interlocutor his blunder; finding it out by himself, his bad humor will not surface, since there will have been neither words nor discussion.

Naturally, practice this silent acceptance, this renunciation of your ideas, only when dealing with your superiors, and when, in your interchanges with inferiors or equals, the matters in question are of little consequence—for we must also envisage our responsibilities toward family, and in all social situations. But a man is rarely bossy everywhere. If he is a tyrant at home, outside the home he is subject to his superiors; if he is inflexible in business, yet will he yield to his wife's demands. Let us take the middle road and conciliate opposites. Let us analyze when and in which cases we are intractable, who are the persons we impose our will upon, and try to reform ourselves.

Let us remember that gentleness is the most powerful moral force. The great spiritual leaders were always infinitely patient toward their rebellious flock, even toward traitors. You will note examples of this in the lives of the saints who exerted the deepest personal influence upon their surroundings: such, for example, were Benoit de Nurcie, Francis of Assisi, Ignatius of Loyola, Vincent de Paul. We never heard them defend their opinions, even during the Councils over which they presided. They were content to state their views. And that sufficed for others to come around, accept, and fall in with their opinions.

Let us try then to acquire this moral authority, which commands respect, rather than resorting to pathetic discourses, grand gestures, and perorations. It seems childish to recommend men to make themselves heard. However, let the tranquillity of our speech not be artificial; on the contrary, let it express the tranquility of our heart. And in this way, having given those around us proof that we speak only advisedly, we will be listened to when we take up an absent person's defence in front of a whole group.

I recommend that you practice tolerance among yourselves. Each man follows the true method for which he is qualified, on condition that he be profoundly sincere. One man may walk the path of sorrow, another that of love, a third that of prayer, etc. They are all in the truth; thus, it is useless for one or the other to boast about his personal path.

We are monks in a monastery; yes, monks inwardly in an invisible monastery. Monks have many subjective temptations equivalent to our objective temptations; on the other hand, they have all sorts of exterior supports, while we have but one support, which is quite personal and hidden: we will stand fast only on condition that we construct for ourselves a firm buttress through incessant corporeal and material renunciations.

August 23, 1914

The influence of any writer, lecturer, or preacher, be he a Bossuet or a St John Chrysostom, exerts itself primarily upon the mental body of his auditors. But from the mental state to the spiritual heart is a far distance. I do not mean to say that we should scorn culture or the enlightenment of a mind. We must grasp any possible means of action. However, they must be kept in their place at the right level.

August 23, 1914

It is painful for me not to be seeing any of you during this tragic period.[2]

We are obliged at this time to perform our independent tasks separately, each in our own way. Let us accept this test with poise, with composure; let us be resolute in accepting to pay this price. Whatever your function may be, fulfill it with all your heart—and even beyond that. Do not fear wearing yourselves out. May those of you who do not have an assigned function find a way of making yourselves useful.

Remember that your spirit battles prior to the body; also afterwards. Expect that battle during your nights, after the diurnal battles of the body. You have to be heroes!

I leave you with this thought of a courageous man; transpose it into the moral world and engrave it into your heart: Kleber has said, "To be a soldier means, when one is hungry, not to eat; when one is thirsty, not to drink; when one is exhausted, to walk; when one cannot move forward any more, to shoulder your wounded comrades."

I envy you, all of you who are endangering yourselves, willing to give up your life several times a day to the final hour—I salute you. To each of you I send my deepest feelings. Your names are ever-present in my thoughts.

August 30, 1914

This particular period is not conducive to critical analyses. Surely you have by now examined your conscience, some before leaving for the front and probable death, others during the dolorous hours of inactivity spent in waiting.

---

[2] World War I.

It is now imperative for you to pray, to surpass yourselves constantly. One hour of prayer is more fruitful than three of discussion; but accomplishing one's work for one minute is still more productive.

All of us have been, are now, and will be on a path; every one knows, has known, and will know one truth; all have received, are receiving, or will receive one life. Among these are many good people; among the good people there are Christians; among Christians we find the true disciples who have followed the more direct and narrower paths, who have known truths that are more and more real, who have received a far more enriching life. Profit from this present period of sacrifices to deepen your experience.

I beseech the Master who made himself our servant to watch over your minds and bodies, to take them along with him by re-enacting for you the "washing of the feet," which will strengthen you during the difficult marches across the fields.

October 1914

We know all our theories well enough by heart; let us put them into practice. None of us occupies first-fiddle chairs or prominent posts; we have received lights that many eminent people have not received; third and finally, we hired ourselves out in the service of the great Farmer. I beg of you, remember these three things. Contemplate their grandeur, their height, and their depth. May these things permeate your acts; may they magnify them. Whether at the front, in the ambulance corps, running errands, or civilian tasks—give your maximum everywhere, all the time, with your whole strength.

After the war, you will be called to other tasks. But during the war let your heart sound the charge, constantly.

Anchor yourself to faith, so that nothing will seem impossible.

I am close to you. I pray with and for you. But I do not ask the Father to protect you. Ask Him to give you His force superabundantly.

I embrace you all with the ardent desire that the fire from the Holy Spirit will descend upon you, that it may transfigure you, confer upon you strength, wisdom, and love.

December 1915

At the end of this dolorous year, let us recapitulate and weigh the efforts we have put forth. Many among you have truly set out well, working in prayer and for love. On the other hand, I notice a certain fatigue, a certain effort in your attitudes. The fresh, airy, wingèd enthusiasm of the beginning has abated slowly, planed down. This is really not quite your fault, because you are not seasoned warhorses, at least not yet; but you are partly to blame, because you have perhaps not quite kept an inner simplicity.

Put all your worries aside for a few hours one day a week. Take a spiritual bath. Go out and see art or nature. Read over some beautiful, edifying pages. Above all, forgetting everything, look through the eyes of your heart. See Jesus in the fields—kind, good, handsome, speaking to the poor, and smiling. Learn how to smile so that your inner joy will be expressed in that manner—because a smile can also be grave. A smile is strength: heaven is not sad; it is Lucifer who suffers melancholy.

Never consider yourselves exiles. The disciple of Jesus is never exiled anywhere, since the adorable Presence accompanies him everywhere. Do we not posses the key to beatitude?

Keep fighting with the assurance that the certitude of an ultimate victory gives you. Seek beauty for a while; it will give you rest from so much searching for the good and the true.

September 1916

You must have noticed, my friends, that in spite of sudden catastrophes, unforeseen promotions, and the innumerable downfalls of which the web of this present dilemma is woven, we are remaining in secondary, rather obscure positions. Had heaven wanted us to occupy important posts, it would have furnished us the necessary faculties. Examples of such promotions exist.

Consequently, this obscurity that our principles order us to cheerfully accept must appear to us not only as the just consequence of our mediocrity, but also as God's decree for us. It is precisely out of this very obscurity that the supernatural seeds received from the divine Gardener will germinate.

These darknesses are dual. Your hearts, my friends, are the tangent point where your own night contacts the night of your fellowman. Dig mine shafts and galleries within yourselves; dig some also into the hearts of your brothers. Your professional life, though remaining paramount and your best means of publicity, may give you the freedom of influencing others in a more direct manner.

I repeat, the best publicity is to be an example: a service rendered operates better than a speech; a kind smile restores serenity upon another's brow faster than a sermon. Besides that, do not fear to give your opinion, even when it is not asked for. You must dare speak even to those who (one surmises in advance) will turn a deaf ear to your voice. Perhaps they will shrug their shoulders, but they will at least have heard.

Test yourselves. Find startling, forcible words to express your ideas concisely. Learn how to anticipate objections, make your interlocutor touch the nothingness of what he believes to be a reality. Because, if there is a void in the center of all things, it is up to you to bring eternal plenitude into it. Moreover, do not try to lead everyone toward the same summit. God is vast enough to offer the appropriate ideal to fulfill and satisfy all aspirations.

You must have an understanding of all things. Your spirits must be untiringly hospitable. Nothing must dishearten you; nothing must seem negligible. Yet, you cannot impose yourself upon anyone. I am aware that as soon as an acquaintance has asked you for information, as soon as you have awakened curiosity or interest in someone, you are responsible for the modifications your light has brought to this individual. Hence, respect the free will of others; beware of directing their consciences; be a sentinel standing watch in the shadows; do not become watch-dogs.

Do not impose your opinion. If your auditor of yesterday has stopped listening to you and scoffs, let him go, but pray for him; ask for the light of truth to shine upon him; do not discontinue this secret intercession until it has borne fruit. Because God, when authorizing you to invoke Him, gives you the right of importuning Him, and also assures you an inviolable seal of secrecy upon what you confide to Him. The spirit of the brother for whom you pray, if you wish it so, will never know he owes you anything.

Thus, alternating between manual effort and spiritual effort, equilibrating verbal information with the silent predication of prayer, you will satisfy the dual duties heaven has honored you with by entrusting them to your care.

Weariness may set in; it is inevitable. I might even say it

is good that it should; it is good that it does, because it becomes the dawn of a rebirth within you. But to feel its weight less, you must accept it.

Nothing here on earth has any definitive importance, since God is here. The only real catastrophe is losing our desire for God.

July 1917

Most of us are tired. And for those who are not, I propose we take a little time off, so we might all sit together on the side of the road under the shade of the apple trees. Let us recall the moments, already now in the distant past, when so many of you left to defend your native soil; let us also recall the moments of former lives when a voice from on high whispered to our spirit the call to divine servitude. May the ebbing flow of our energies ascend to its source, to the hollow of the eternal rock where the doves of the *Song of Songs* are nestling.

Let us remember the day when, of our own free will, we dedicated ourselves totally to the service of Christ, when we entered into the free-for-all of existence, of being, and into that of war. This took place without words, so it was well done. The solitude, the bareness of the earthly scenery, the lack of pomp in the intimate acts of our lives, call around us, into our inner heaven, the company of angels, the magnificences of the divine City, and the true glories sounded by the trumpets of the Last Judgment.

That artless little moment when you and I gave ourselves to Jesus is, in reality, the tiny point of light that, through its lens, sums up the immense splendor of the sun at the meridian. At that moment my spirit, your spirit, which had been searching for the Shepherd, perhaps for centuries, had finally encountered Jesus. At that moment, Jesus looked at me. Made ready through the patient ministrations of angels, I was able to see him. I saw my Master, my Lord, my Friend. I met my ideal face to face, and the reality infinitely surpassed my wildest imaginings. In attendance at this audience were the spirits of ancestors and of descendants, the spirit of the people, the creatures with whom I had had to converse; the guardian angels and the mixed genii, and also my tempters (pitiless agents of my purification), as also my future tempters, whom I will have to convert. Could I help giving myself wholly in a final exuberance?

My consciousness perceived but a dwarfed image of this brief drama. My intellect thought it could influence my will. But both obeyed the superconscious exaltation of my unknown self, whose terrestrial personality is but a barely structured organ.

The vocation that makes us slaves of Jesus, the accepted slavery that makes us free because it progressively unites us to the supreme Slave of Love, forms the binding knot of such a dramatic pathos that its strains must resound through the remainder of our existence. That is why, during our hours of meditation, we should relive that moment inwardly, celebrate and commemorate it in utmost privacy.

Mystical plighting of our troth—as a perpetual pledge in the world in which our spirit moves—implies a parallel perpetuity upon the terrestrial world. Just as that betrothal becomes a transplantation of all our spiritual roots once and for all before Christ, so must the virtue of this pact penetrate our whole being, provide new strength to all of our substances, orient even the least of our instinctive movements toward the divine goal—thereby rendering us impassable to bruises, even to the rack. For this, an unceasing strain is needed, a constant, intense aspiration from our affective powers. Meditation does not suffice. To systematically exercise our will does not suffice. *An incendiary love, an all-consuming love, is necessary.*

That lassitude may overcome those who have not yet received a glance from the Shepherd is conceivable. But we must not flinch, we cannot give in to these lapses.

Because we have given ourselves to Christ, we have stepped out from the domain of justice, and consequently from the domain of injustice also. We have entered into the domain of love, where the fusion of justice and injustice operates. From now on, why should it matter whether we suffer as obscure victims of petty vexations and stingy pesterings, or as heroes ablaze in glory, since in any case we cannot and should not suffer but for the sake of love? Or rather, we cannot and must not be anything else but happy to suffer, whether from justice or injustice. And to top it all, we should be supremely happy to suffer *because of* apparent injustices. Whatever work we do must be done passionately, since all our works consecrated to Jesus are transmuted by him into gems for eternity.

Whatever our task may be, let us become accustomed never to see evil. First of all, let us never believe that injustice is aimed at us personally; secondly, let us never consider injustices except as forms of restitution—more direct than others—from prior depredations we once wrought upon weaker creatures. And above all, let us sustain an inner dialogue with Jesus.

Within the unknown, unfathomed depths of the self, the voluntary spiritual act that consecrated our vocation constitutes a pact binding us forever. To fail to vivify our recollection of it, to fail to attempt to enlarge or to fathom the understanding or consciousness we have of it, does not in any way weaken this obligation. Our negligence in this matter merely renders it less affective and more difficult to uphold—for in time it becomes more and more difficult. On the contrary, we must often contemplate the memory of this noble tribute. For the phenomena that occur in the order of nature dissolve in the course of their span of time and are diluted in space. But those in whose generation a factor of eternity intervenes, remain unassailable and retain their primitive vigor; they enjoy the privilege of immanent presence; outside time, at the center of space, they remain; and they continue to be accessible to the visits that our fervor wishes to make to them.

If, then, I prove able to maintain an immutable calm in my heart through the control of my native versatility, the divine presence will not find any obstacles preventing its inexpressible lights from being shed upon my whole being; and if at the same time I plunge my heart, greedy by birth for glory and grandeur, into the constant humiliations of obscure labors, the light will not only illumine it, but will pour into it in overflowing streams, and—for my eyes—clothe this miserable world with its splendor and serenity.

Hence, I would like to see you, my friends, seek refuge more frequently in those caverns of the eternal rock where the shocks of howling gales cannot reach. It is possible in the midst of the most tormented, charged existence to maintain oneself in a steadfast inner peace. Other men have been able to attain it. Why not you? All you have to do is change the abode of your heart; or rather, in the words of the gospel, choose the object of your love in the immutable. Do you not know that if the Father so willed it, his reign would be established this instant? And have you not experienced a thousand times that the hardships you endured, not excepting the least comprehensible among them, have in the end always resulted in providing you a supplement of forces and a greater capacity for happiness?

September 1917

If we possessed wisdom, if we knew how to conduct ourselves so as never to disrupt the evolutionary harmony of a single being, neither laws, nor the Law would have any reason for being. They exist because we do not comply.

The law is: "Love ye one another." Laws are the innumerable commentaries pertaining to all the civil and religious situations where men, socially-grouped, may find themselves. They are often narrow commentaries, seemingly opposed in their principle. They are often vexatious, and even formulated by selfishness and tyrannies (and thus frequently instigators of revolts); yet the disciple knows he must abstain from judging. The Master's recommendation should suffice, as it stands, if we want to take the shortest route and apply the power of certitude which ignorance of the law possesses. But very few are capable of this supernatural blindness. Let us, then, find together the motives for obedience.

We are always the subordinate of someone, or the captive of something. Lucifer himself, the freest of beings—since he is the perpetual rebel—remains the slave of his pride. Hence, our position is that we must submit to our fate, even as we extract from this fatality its best and most expedient means. Yielding to the inevitable, submitting to a state of things that binds us, seems to be the regime that destiny inflicts upon us in order to compel—to grind—us into submission. It is through this arduous gymnastic that we learn obedience. Each act of obedience is a paltry seed that later on will produce the vigorous shoots and paradisiacal flowers of dedicated self-sacrifice.

Obedience is the primary school of renunciation; it is abnegation by mandate. Spontaneous renunciation follows. It is evident that it is because obedience irks us that it yields spiritual results. An order invariably creates work, consequently it always develops our organs or our faculties: whether the order be vexatious or meaningless, no work is useless. Even the artificial occupations that the indolent invent to fill their time have their utility. But beyond these natural consequences, obedience—because it bends the very core of our pride into submission, because it castigates our sloth—reaches the very principle of our self-will, and consequently lifts us toward abandonment in God.

It is evident that to obey out of fear of punishment only procures the ordinary fruit of any activity. The disciple must obey for mystical motives. Because there is no earthly power except the one that comes from God, in the final analysis any civil, political, or religious authority is but one form of divine authority, even if perhaps a remote and often unrecognizable one—given how far it has diverged from its principle. To be precise, the disciple's faith enables him to perceive God behind the non-commissioned officer, behind the policeman, behind the bus driver. And, because of this faith, the angels of the One who (being the omnipotent Lord) wanted to become like the least of slaves, reorganize and reassemble on a new plane all the fateful cogs that lead to the petty tyrannies against which we grumble.

To the one who has given himself solemnly and definitively to Christ, all events, things, and beings with which his destiny puts him into contact undergo a mysterious transformation in their essence, if not in their form—so that they become for this disciple the exact orders of divine will in his regard. And insofar as his vocation has been lofty and his renunciation profound, he can (without indulging here in rhetorical figures) catch a glimpse of God in the form of his temporal rulers. A man still held by the external, however, remains subject to the regime of mixed bodies and compound forces that in themselves are prey to the continual struggle between duty and selfishness.

*March 1919*

It pains me to incite you to redouble your efforts, and speak always of hardships, and not of relaxations. I certainly would like to invite you to some exquisite banquets. But we are at work, faced with a very hard task. Should you fall forty times a day, you must rise as many. Take courage, life is so short; also, you are well aware and know by experience that heaven sustains us when needful.

*December 1919*

You possess the distinct privilege of feeling at times the divine Presence. It is essential that you speak to many. Train yourselves to move, to stir them—not by eloquence, but by the silent intensity of your own emotion. If, when closeted in your room, you do not weep often upon your imperfections, you will never be able to bring others to tears over theirs. Neither beautiful periods of euphoria nor ponderous books can move hearts. What does stir them are words falling from pure and ardent lips. Notice how the directors of souls speak sparingly and simply, yet each syllable of theirs is charged, surcharged, oversaturated, with tears, yearnings, flames, and sorrows. Disseminate then, upon all people, the sparks of that incandescent fire which shines within you, even when exchanging commonplace words.

You have noticed how the life of the servants of God is paved with suffering. But none among us suffers more than any other. Why? Is it because we fail to ask the Father for this daily bread for our soul? Is it due to some new or inexplicable privilege? It is not for us to know. But should not our special status spark our energies? Let your annoyances and banal tribulations pass unnoticed. You are marching in the direction of God, and you are aware of it. Hence, march. The final victory is assured, whatever may be the denouement, the sudden turns of fate of the conflict. If you are not sufficiently aware that it is Christ who leads you, it means that you are too involved with yourselves, personally and figuratively. Go out more, break your habits—did not Jesus sally forth from his Father's house for you, for us all?

September 1920

Never forget to give thanks to God; never forget that the best thanksgiving is making a promise of better serving our Master. Let us anchor our humility upon deeper pilings. Jesus chose an ass for his public entry. The ass bears a cross on his back, yet is satisfied to feast upon meager thistles. Let us be the "asses," the "fools" of the Lord. And if perchance our Master places relics upon our shoulders, let us still think of ourselves as being beasts of burden by remaining in the background at the end of the line.

I send you, dear beloved brothers, my embrace—a sign of the union, or rather the unity, that joins us together around our leader, Christ.

January 1921

Cost what it may, regardless of anything, we must hold fast by training each feature of our faces never to express anything but calm, cordiality, affectionate goodwill, and kindness. As this result is impossible unless our heart is in that state, this is an excellent means to attain an imperturbable inner equilibrium.

I am well aware that the extent of the task to be accomplished rather tests your composure. Keep your equanimity. In one's interior life, the slightest local effort produces a general effect. Had the disciple enough perseverance and depth, the absolute realization of a single gospel counsel pertaining to a particular point would suffice to bring him to perfection. However, we must understand the weakness of our character, which has need of diversity.

I embrace you, my friends, holding you close to my heart in the luminous shadow of our Master.

February 1921

The beginning of the calendar year is also the beginning of a spiritual cycle. In spite of the hardships that destiny has heaped upon many of you, I wish each new blow of fate would encourage you, would seem to you to be a mark of heaven's confidence, a proof of the trust of heaven, which puts its best workmen to the hardest test.

It is essential that we definitively accept as an experienced truth, as an axiom, that our sole reason for being lies in our acceptance of everything that less enlightened men repel— even in our search for everything they fear. We should be able to say deliberately, when facing life: "If I proceed thus and so, I will evade all difficulties; consequently, I must proceed in this other manner, since my role—the role I chose— is to straighten the crooked, to smooth the rough, to bring light into the dark corners where men do not venture."

July 1921

Nothing matters but being distracted from God, who desires that we submit to any exigencies with gladness.

Therefore, try to remain silent and smile when your business goes awry, when your close associates become demanding or ungrateful, when your employees serve you badly, when anyone tyrannizes you. Then, and only then, will your spirit enter into the kingdom, and will you find your prayers answered.

December 1922

I would like to find you always dauntless, fearless, before suffering, so that none of its shards scratch the diamond of your faith. You must gird the belt of your faith. Never must anyone penetrate your defenses; protect yourself at all cost. This has to be done in the humblest manner, by diminishing yourself to the least spiritual dimensions. The sole stable, lasting faith is humility. Thus, any occasion given you to suffer will become grounds for gladness.

Remember Jesus's admonition: "When you fast, anoint your hair and wear your party clothes!"[3] This is the true maxim. Seclude yourself in a closet if ever you have the weakness to weep. Whatever may his trials or his anxieties be, the soldier of Christ remains in a blissful state.

Consolidate your faith, it will never let you down, in any world.

January 1923

I hope you will become conscious of the perpetual presence of Jesus near you. This presence is constant: every second of time, and from all points of space. This presence is called the Son—and the Son, our Christ Jesus, is perpetually here. He never leaves any of us. He stands at the side of the prince as well as by the vagabond, at the side of the savage as well as by the genius, at the side of the criminal as well as

---

[3] Matthew 6:17, paraphrased.

by the saint. He sees everything. He hears everything. He discerns everything. And since we have loved this formidable Being, let us be logical in our heart—let this love become our sole motive and our total strength. Let us know that our Lord looks at us and smiles at us. Let this certitude become our whole law, our whole scripture, our whole beatitude.

May 1923

During our conversations, I have spoken often of prayer. I have stressed and insisted upon the immense importance of prayer. Let me remind you that before falling asleep one should recollect and pray for two or three minutes from the bottom of one's heart, from that tenuous state of liaison with God that mystics call the summit of the spirit. These particular prayers are often granted. We all prefer praying with fervor, with enthusiasm and joy—that is understandable. But the poor little demand, so bare, so short, so feeble, is probably gathered up by our Friend with more bliss. In fact, it is the quality of our conduct during the day that determines the quality of the evening prayer.

Very dear friends, to whom I owe my only joys, I embrace you with all my heart in the name of our beloved Master.

November 1923

You have learned through your own experience that the best means of obtaining natural and durable results is still to struggle against oneself; or rather, to attain mastery over oneself. I am perfectly well aware how, when cornered and worn down by the constant petty annoyances of life, you let yourself become irritated, even to the point of anger. You must absolutely cure yourself of that. I would like you to amass enough strength to emulate what I once saw a soldier of Christ accomplish who, wanting to overcome a fault, took a pledge not to fail for forty days, and who in fact did not succumb.

Control your gestures, control your facial expressions, control your speech. And if perchance you cannot prevent your heart from being discontented, at least see to it that nothing will come of it, or be read upon your face.

December 1923

Barrenness, or what is commonly known as periods of aridity, may be nothing more than exhaustion owing to our clumsy efforts. Remember that in the spiritual domain, as well as in the physical, the most useful effort is a supple, flexible one. Smile even when you are overcoming a fault. In deploying perfect force, the effort goes unnoticed.

When you are moved by suffering, deny yourself one thing, and pray. Yet, do not abstain unduly or overmuch. Skip a meal, pass up an outing or a pleasure. But do not ruin your health with penance—that is not your right. Moreover, do not deprive in this way anyone entrusted to your care. You do not have that right either. The only organ you must subject to fasting within you is that of selfishness, pride, vanity, avarice, anger, and sloth—these six being but one.

October 1925

Were we truly his servants, our flame would be sufficiently ardent to overcome our laziness, our timidity, our negligence; we would not need anyone to remind us what must be done.

You know that before God, an act is only as good as its spontaneity; what we have to do, we have to do of our own free will. Brochures, pamphlets, meetings, visits, reunions, and talks are but means—expressions of our faith. But if we want that faith to live, we must feed it by acts.

December 24, 1925

I ask you once again, and with the greatest insistence, to test everything I say to you with the word of Christ, to follow only Christ, to follow me only insofar as you are certain that I am in Christ. Moreover, heaven judges our intentions primarily, before weighing our acts.

Then, let us each remain at our post, calmly and peacefully, mindful to act with the certitude our supernatural confidence and love give us. May he who willingly came as the poorest and most abandoned among the children of men kindly receive our unworthy adoration and take pity on the paucity of our heart, and on the desolate solitude of our selfishness.

# Further Letters

Your prayer to God moved me profoundly. You asked heaven to send its unfortunates your way; and the needy came in droves—the sick, the stray sheep, the harlots, large families of hungry people. This work was grueling, but it also had its joys. A test, when asked from heaven, is tough as leather. God does not grant it to us unless we ask Him from our whole heart with tears, and unless we are strong enough to bear it. If that test is granted us, we must be courageous, always ready to accept the sacrifices it entails, even when (and especially when) those we are called to serve do not seem to merit it. However, we must be prudent and very conscientious; especially, before taking any action, we must refer our mode of conduct entirely to God. That way, we will rarely become the dupes of the Adversary.

Remember that we can walk only towards error or toward truth, toward the Adversary or towards Christ. After all, we are all proceeding towards truth, and that should be immensely consoling to us, and proof as well of the unfaltering, infinite love of the Father. But those who remain too long in error delay the return of all humanity to the fold. Because of them, the indescribable sufferings of our Lord are prolonged.

We may possess vast erudition, a remarkable intelligence, have aspirations toward the ideal. But all these earthly gifts may lead to error, and to such a degree that we begin incarnating error even into our sentiments, our thoughts, our acts. Yet one thing alone is necessary, the only one that leads to truth, that alone is accessible to all: it is the blend of charity, humility, and prayer.

July 1913

You wish you had more time to devote to your interior life. This is part of our personal difficulties, from which we must learn how to extricate ourselves. We must begin by reading a few lines from the gospel every day. Yes, every day we must multiply our meager efforts. We must lay stone upon stone, because in the end the totality becomes a considerable edifice.

We are not saints. That is one of the main reasons we should strive to become saints. It is especially by practicing charity, by practicing love, that we will advance. To help our fellow man is the whole crux and foundation; the rest will inevitably follow.

September 1914

You must have spent many agonizing hours as a hundred thousand bonds are being torn apart with blood![4] How many days such as these have yet to be endured! Still, it is well to have suffered, received, undergone, borne these wounds. Our capacity to love expands because of it. It is elevated, becomes deeper and loftier. It enables us to transmute our love by multiplying its effective realizations.

But this is hardly the time for theories. Action will keep you busy! Remember that in the midst of the battle, during your ordeals as a soldier, nothing will protect your family, nothing will restore their strength, better than to put your whole heart into the work at hand. You know it; but I have to repeat it to you as I have experienced it. It is easy to

---

[4] Written just months after WWI began.

believe that to be torn in two by thinking of our absent ones helps them more. But it is quite otherwise: it is more effective to throw yourself wholeheartedly into the successive duties of each minute. So yes, think of your loved ones, pray for them; but don't pass your days tearing your spirit apart.

October 1914

You must learn how to will. So, will. There are two ways of expressing will. The first and most common is by tightening the jaw, pursing the lips, and scowling. The second, much healthier and less lopsided, is to will with a smile. In the former, the lever's fulcrum is our self-awareness, or pride. In the latter, it is the consciousness we have of Jesus. Experiment with patience.

*To a friend who had just lost his father.*

January 3, 1915

I cannot imagine that you are in need of consolation. Keep your strength, find strength for your poor dear mother, certainly more broken up than are you by this blow, expected as it had been.

What can I say to you? If you will permit my speaking of myself, I can confess that never had I felt so close to the Certitude than the day my most beloved, saintly, angelic wife passed away. It seems to me that to those of us who, though unworthy, have received some rays of enlightenment, the same pains that lacerate other hearts cauterize our wounds, shore us up, elevate us toward the realm of serenity.

I hold you close to my heart.

January 16, 1915

You take things too much to heart. Remember that they are what heaven permits them to be—unless they happen to fall into the domain of our responsibility.

Remember also that, as was said in the eighteenth century, the honest, virtuous man must make virtue appear to be attractive. So smile, do not be angry with the poor brutes who surround you. That you might not attempt to better them is possible; though in truth you should. But I grant you it is extremely difficult. Try, at least, to consider them with loving compassion.

You see, when there is a mountain to climb, you must approach it gently.

1922

We must guard against the innate tendency to unload upon others the care and solace that the sick and unfortunate require. It would be preferable, even at the risk of not succeeding quite so quickly, to take care of those in our charge ourselves by sustaining our proceedings through spiritual fasts. Our Association will fulfill its aim more and more if we give priority to the mystical counterpart of our material charities. First comes heaven, then the unfortunate, then us, in that straight line. The norm is that this line must not be broken. Hence, each one must consolidate it by undertaking personally the ministrations necessary for the poor (job, money, clothing) by means both of physical efforts and spiritual acts.

August 25, 1924

These are hard times indeed. This year we freeze and flounder under a colossal weight, which an opaque and heavy atmosphere accentuates more than would sunny skies.

We must never write unless we have something to say; then say it with all the strength, simplicity, and clarity we can muster.

Forgive me for acting the schoolmaster, and please do not take my remarks as unassailable axioms.

Do your best and pray. It is still Christ who will teach you the best writing.

Affectionately yours

July 16, 1925

Madame,

I would like to see you more profoundly resigned to the will of God, by having more confidence in Him. He has recalled your spouse; why should you be tormented about his destiny on the other side? God prepares for our birth on earth. He furnishes us parents and all sorts of sustenance. Would you then believe that for that other birth, the one that follows upon our earthly demise, He would abandon us all alone in some invisible desert?

Your husband has understood your tenderness and he still feels it, be certain of it. Do not overburden yourself, for the time being, with materialistic concerns in his memory. Maintain toward him an open, inwardly calm attitude, devoid of acts and gestures that, rather than liberating his spirit, would keep him earthbound. Conjugal love is primarily a union of souls. When the body is there, and the person is there, life in common has to be lived in all that material, family, and social existence entails. When the one spouse's body is no longer here, strivings toward sanctity and kindness on the part of the remaining spouse are the surest and only way of helping the one who has left.

Finally, know that now your husband is resting; you need not worry about his state.

At this time you must rest. To take care of one's body is a duty. Look into the future with assurance and calm. God will never abandon you.

Accept, Madame, my very sincere wishes and my respectful homage.

⊕

One must make use of dry periods; it is good husbandry. There comes a time, after having served Him out of a sense of duty, when we begin to take pleasure in serving God. As egoism is immortal, this pure pleasure becomes, if prolonged, a pleasure of its own. Then heaven takes it away from us, sends us drought, to purify this reflection of His light in us. And from fervor to languor, we slowly descend the slopes of true humility into the valley at the bottom of which the disciple finds himself at peace: a joyous, permanent peace. Having little left of his own will, everything has become, not indifferent (as Buddhists believe), but agreeable, because he discerns in everything the means of serving God.

So continue your examinations working successively, from the outside in:

your outer senses: your eyes, ears, sensations;
your inner senses: judgment, critiquing, meditation;
your inner self: the light of the soul communicating with the Word.

⊕

I do not write to you very often either, though I am quite aware of your fatigues, and how daily life weighs upon you pitilessly.

Your crossing of the desert is drawing to an end; it has been very hard. We know well, however, that we each have our own desert, where sun, hardships, and highwaymen are proportioned to our particular need. No desert is worse than another. It is only that the one we cross seems to be the worst.

Your household is cumbersome too, my dear old fellow. But you are not the only one. We all have to gird our loins, square our shoulders, and accept responsibilities.

Upon our Atlas and upon our backs
Let us load, load and heap, the heavy burdens.

You see, I am not serious, but I embrace you with all my heart.

⊕

The gods you serve through your art are like all of us: they too are servants of the supreme deity, of Christ. What art needs most at this time are artists who, by interpreting the gods through the flame of their heart, will lead them back to God. Just as, in literature, many musical compositions are pagan—and some that bear a Christian label, such as [Wagner's] *Parzival*, are more pagan than the others. But, fortunately, in art, once you have mastered the craft, feeling wins out. Play as a Christian, for Christ, for the Virgin, and your bow will transfigure the most sensual harmonies.

It is of course admitted that an artist needs passions, women, and the rest; yes—because they are atheists. But if the artist is a Christian—or, rather, a saint—these outer stimuli will be replaced by the inner stimulus of divine love, prayer, and sacrifice. You must be able to get emotions that are pure even out of the most maudlin music. It can be done.

Uplift your interpretation of a work of art. By elevating it toward the Absolute, you will at the same time elevate the work you are interpreting. A work is alive—never forget it. Always look higher, always look deeper. Parallels meet at infinity. That is what Baudelaire meant when attempting to compare Delacroix, Ingres, and Daumier in one of his "Salons." His conclusion? "Let us love all three."

⊕

Dear Madame,

I understand you; I too love dogs and always have some near me. Yours had an admirable head, and eyes... The dog is a friend, the friend of man. He is to be found with man everywhere there are men in the universe. We must have some, and speak to them, and help them live. Their destiny follows ours; they do suffer and they accompany us. Do not worry about yours. Bury him in a little white pine box, wrap him well—corpses need a sign of affection. And God will not find it strange that you speak to Him of this humble creature. If it is too late to take care of his burial, you can always pray. You will impart calm to him naturally. You know—or rather, one is never sufficiently aware—that God never takes exception to anything we may do that springs from our loving confidence.

With my most respectful and fervent wishes, Madame.

www.ingramcontent.com/pod-product-compliance
Lightning Source LLC
Chambersburg PA
CBHW020332100426
42812CB00029B/3098/J